COMMUNITY
COLLEGE
FACT
BOOK

American Council on Education/
American Association of Community
and Junior Colleges/Macmillan
Series on Higher Education

COMMUNITY

COLLEGE

FACT

BOOK

Compiled by
ELAINE EL-KHAWAS, DEBORAH J. CARTER
and CECILIA A. OTTINGER

American Association of Community and Junior Colleges

American Council on Education Macmillan Publishing Company
NEW YORK
Collier Macmillan Publishers
LONDON

The American Council on Education/Macmillan Series on Higher Education

Macmillan Publishing Company
866 Third Avenue, New York, N.Y. 10022

Collier Macmillan Canada, Inc.

Library of Congress Catalog Card Number: 87-37232

Printed in the United States of America

printing number
1   2   3   4   5   6   7   8   9   10

Library of Congress Cataloging in Publication Data

El-Khawas, Elaine H.
     Community college fact book / compiled by Elaine El-Khawas,
Deborah J. Carter, and Cecilia A. Ottinger.
        p.   cm. — (American Council on Education/American Association
of Community and Junior Colleges/Macmillan series on higher
education)
     Bibliography: p.
     Includes index.
     ISBN 0-02-900941-3
     1. Community colleges—United States—Statistics. I. Carter,
Deborah J. II. Ottinger, Cecilia A. III. American Council on
Education. IV. American Association of Community and Junior
Colleges. V. Title. VI. Title: Community college fact book.
VII. Series.
LB2328.E47 1988
378'.1543'0973—dc19   87–37232
                                                                  CIP

AACJC Board of Directors

Executive Staff

Dale Parnell, *President and Chief Executive Officer*

James A. Gollattscheck, *Executive Vice President and Association Treasurer*

Connie Odems, *Vice President for Professional Services and Association Secretary*

Frank Mensel, *Vice President/Director for Federal Relations*

Daniel D. Savage, *Vice President for Communication Services*

Academy and Commission Presidents

Lex D. Walters, President
Piedmont Technical College
Chair, Presidents Academy

Donald J. Donato, President
Niagara County Community College
Chair, Commission on Small and/or Rural Community Colleges

William J. Mann, Chancellor
The Metropolitan Community Colleges
Chair, Urban Community Colleges Commission

John E. Ravekes, President
Essex Community College
Chair, AACJC/ACCT Joint Commission on Federal Relations

Ernest L. Boyer, President
Carnegie Foundation for the Advancement of Teaching
Chair, Commission on the Future of the Community Colleges

Bob F. Owen, President
Florida College
Chair, Commission on Independent Colleges

ACE Board of Directors

Contents

II. Planning Information   41

Foreword

Community, technical, and junior colleges now make up the largest single segment of America's postsecondary educational system, enrolling over 50 percent of the nation's entering college freshmen and 43 percent of the total undergraduate population. Questions surrounding the operation and impact of these institutions are thus central to an understanding of the contemporary American higher education scene. How many community college students successfully transfer to baccalaureate-granting institutions? How does the demographic profile of community college students differ from the profile of students at four-year colleges and universities? How have costs and revenues at community colleges changed over the past 10 years? These and other questions are often asked by researchers and students, yet few information sources provide relevant data in response.

This first edition of the *Community College Fact Book,* produced jointly by the American Council on Education and the American Association of Community and Junior Colleges, addresses this information problem by highlighting current data on community, technical, and junior colleges. Drawing from a variety of sources, the *Fact Book* summarizes trends in enrollment, student characteristics and achievement, institutional finances, and administration. In addition, Part II of the *Fact Book* details social and demographic indicators bearing on the future of community colleges. These indicators include trends in the educational attainment of the population, ethnic and age-related changes in the overall makeup of the population, and shifts in the labor force. Besides providing a descriptive analysis of community, technical, and junior colleges, the data presented in the *Fact Book* portray the larger social environment in which they operate.

Though the *Fact Book* is not exhaustive, it does provide researchers and policymakers with a convenient source of data bearing on issues surrounding community, technical, and junior colleges today. We hope that this edition will be the first in a series that periodically presents updated statistics on this important segment of American higher education.

Robert H. Atwell
President, American Council on Education

Dale Parnell
President, American Association
of Community and Junior Colleges

Introduction

A recent essay in the *Chronicle of Higher Education* carried the title "The Invisible Community Colleges." To a much greater extent than those of us dedicated to the egalitarian wing of higher education would like to admit, the author was correct. In spite of the historically unparalleled growth in both number of institutions and students enrolled, many educational and governmental leaders continue to overlook the critical importance and scale of this sector. The 1987 report of the Carnegie Foundation for the Advancement of Teaching and Learning, "College: The Undergraduate Experience in America," ignored the community, technical, and junior colleges even though they enroll 43 percent of the country's undergraduate population. Other examples of benign neglect are numerous. For years the Center for Education Statistics at the U.S. Department of Education has published annual compilations of academic degrees conferred, omitting the associate degree even though it is second in popularity only to the bachelor's degree. Likewise, the Census Bureau does not include the associate degree in its listing of degrees attained, and as a result there is no reliable count of associate degrees earned in the United States. Even worse, the Bureau's Current Population Series surveys undercount enrollment in two-year institutions by more than 2 million students because of methodological flaws.

America's community, technical, and junior colleges have played a leading role in the expansion of postsecondary education after World War II. In 1946 there were 663 junior colleges, half of which were private, predominantly church-related schools. Now there are approximately 1,200 institutions, the vast majority of which (over 80 percent) are publicly supported colleges serving local communities.

As the colleges grew in number, so did the number of scholars writing about the community college movement. Thousands of books and journal articles have been published, documenting administrative and educational practices. Yet relatively few information resources provide accurate and timely data. Those scholars seeking answers to the questions of "how many" or "how much" often find only scattered, incomplete, or outdated information.

The *Community College Fact Book*, though not exhaustive, was compiled in response to the need for a brief, accurate source of statistical information on community colleges. Drawing upon a variety of published and unpublished resources, the *Community College Fact Book* summarizes selected data on enrollment, funding, students, faculty, finances, and staffing. The *Fact Book* also presents data related to overall trends in population growth, employment, and educational attainment, thus drawing the parameters of the larger socioeconomic environment in which community colleges operate. The statistical portrait emerging in the data highlights several of the key issues facing community college leaders today.

Enrollment Trends

One issue facing community, junior, and technical colleges is the prospect of stabilized and perhaps declining enrollment. Enrollment growth at community colleges has tapered off dramatically in the past decade. While enrollments increased by almost 180 percent from 1966 through 1977, they grew by only 19 percent between 1976 and 1987. During the next 5 years enrollments at two-year institutions are expected to decline slightly as a result of the decrease in the number of individuals in the prime college-going age group, 18–24 years of age. On the other hand, projecting college enrollments has proven to be an especially risky endeavor, as many forecasters of the late 1970s can attest. Relatively small increases in the percentage of adults starting or returning to college can have a major impact on higher education enrollments.

Moreover, general projections do not tell the whole story. Other data presented in the *Community College Fact Book* indicate that enrollment trends will vary between different student populations. Although projections indicate a decrease in the number of full-time students over the next 5 years, the number of part-time students is actually expected to increase. Enrollment variations may also emerge between different regions of the country, as the population of the United States continues to shift toward the South and the West. Another pertinent variable is ethnicity; community colleges may experience growing minority enrollments as the proportion of minorities among elementary and high school students coming up the educational pipeline increases. Finally, the opportunity to enroll greater proportions of older students (those beyond the traditional college-age cohort of 18–24) may present itself as the overall educational attainment of the population increases. Prior research, not summarized in this *Fact Book,* clearly indicates that the more education a person has, the more likely it is that he or she will seek out and enroll in adult-education activities.

Thus, anticipated enrollment declines may not be uniform throughout. Some regions of the country may be more affected than others, and while some segments of the student population will diminish in size, others may grow. Much will depend on the response of community college leaders to the needs of part-time, minority, and older students.

Student Characteristics

Several of the tables indicate that community, junior, and technical colleges enroll a student population that differs on average from the student body at four-year colleges and universities. On the whole, community college students have lower socioeconomic backgrounds than their counterparts at baccalaureate-granting institutions. Students at community colleges are also less likely than four-year college students to aspire to bacalaureate or higher degrees. Data collected in the "High School and Beyond" study, for example, reveal that 59 percent of the high school seniors who plan to earn a bachelor's degree enroll in four-year colleges immediately after graduation, while only 16 percent enroll in public community colleges. In addition, community college students begin their postsecondary education with lower levels of academic achievement. Only 9 percent of the high school seniors with an A average attend community colleges in the first year after graduation; in contrast, 44 percent of these students attend public four-year colleges, and 27 percent attend private four-year colleges. Conversely, community colleges enroll 11 percent of the high school seniors with a D average, while four-year colleges enroll less than 1 percent.

In reviewing these figures, it must be remembered that they reflect average trends and that community colleges enroll large numbers of academically able and ambitious students. Nonetheless, community colleges provide access for a disproportionately large share of students whose educational goals or academic backgrounds render them unlikely candidates for admission to four-year colleges and universities. The enrollment of low-achieving students, many of whom wish to transfer to a four-year institution, is particularly significant; in admitting these students and providing the remediation and support services needed for success at the postsecondary level, community colleges undertake one of the most difficult tasks facing higher education today.

Student Outcomes

A related theme deals with student outcomes. How many community college students complete full programs of study? How many transfer to baccalaureate-granting institutions? Do students who complete a two-year associate degree program earn more than students who do not continue their education beyond the high school diploma? This *Fact Book* provides partial answers to these questions by summarizing the proportion of community college graduates who transfer, the persistence of high school graduates who enroll in community colleges, the number of associate degrees conferred in 1985, and the median incomes of persons who have completed 1–3 years of college. The data on student persistence are of particular interest. They indicate that high school graduates entering community colleges are less likely than their counterparts at four-year institutions to be enrolled 1½ years after matriculation. This situation may reflect any number of factors, including the lower average academic ability of community college students, the fact that fewer community college entrants aspire to baccalaureate or higher degrees, or the tendency (documented elsewhere) of many community college students to enroll infrequently on a stop-in and stop-out basis.

These outcome figures should be viewed only as rough indices. Data collection agencies usually focus on cross-sectional rather than longitudinal analyses, providing information on the number of students enrolled at any one time and not on their progress toward degree or vocational goals. Outcome data that are available often provide an incomplete or spurious picture. For example, data on the number of degrees conferred may be an accurate measure of the number of students who complete full programs of study, but they provide no information on the number of students who fulfill their educational goals without earning a degree. Similarly, transfer rates are significantly underestimated if they are calculated solely on the basis of the number of associate degree recipients who go on to baccalaureate-granting institutions; many students who intend to transfer do so prior to completing associate degree requirements. A more complete picture of student outcomes awaits further research into the actual goals of students and more rigorous student follow-up studies.

Financial Data

In comparison to student outcome data, information on college finances is much more complete. Several points can be drawn from the financial data presented in the *Community College Fact Book:*

- Community colleges are heavily dependent on state governments for financial support. State funds account for almost 50 percent of college revenues, followed (in order of magnitude) by local funds, tuition charges, and federal funds. Private gifts and endowments account for only 1 percent of total revenues.
- Although community colleges receive a disproportionately large share (91 percent) of local funds earmarked for higher education, they receive only 19 percent of state funding to higher education and less than 10 percent of federal higher education funds.
- Federal support for public community, technical, and junior colleges dropped nearly 17 percent between Fall 1985 and Fall 1986, while state and local funds remained constant.
- Current fund expenditures per full-time-equivalent (FTE) student are significantly lower at community, junior, and technical colleges than they are at four-year colleges and universities. In addition, the growth rate of these expenditures (in constant dollars) is lower at community colleges than at baccalaureate-granting

institutions; between 1970 and 1985, per-student expenditures at community colleges increased by only 2 percent, compared to 15 percent at four-year colleges and universities.

The data indicate, in short, that community colleges represent a financially efficient segment of higher education, educating 43 percent of the nation's undergraduates for a disproportionately small share of state and federal higher education monies. At the same time the colleges have managed to minimize growth in spending per FTE student over the past 15 years.

Staffing

One of the major trends in community college staffing—and one that may be partially responsible for the low per-student expenditures mentioned earlier—is the widespread use of part-time faculty, who constitute a slight majority of community college instructors. In addition, the number of part-time faculty has grown at a significantly higher rate than the number of full-time faculty or the number of administrators. Between 1976 and 1986 the number of part-time faculty increased by 47 percent, compared to a 26 percent increase in the number of full-timers and a 36 percent increase in the size of the administrative and professional staff. The use of part-time faculty is a firmly established and growing practice at community, junior, and technical colleges.

Caveats and Further Sources of Information

The data presented in this first edition of the *Community College Fact Book* provide indicators of enrollment trends, student characteristics, student outcomes, institutional finances, and staffing patterns. Other items are covered as well, including student attitudes toward social issues, faculty salaries, and national trends in employment, educational attainment, and population growth.

To be sure, the *Fact Book* will not satisfy all the information needs of those seeking data on community colleges; no one resource is capable of that. The reader seeking further statistical information can turn to several library resources, including the *American Statistics Index*, the *Statistical Reference Index*, and ERIC's *Resources in Education*. Nonetheless, the *Community College Fact Book* performs the valuable service of collecting much of the national data that are available. Though these data have their limitations—especially in the area of student outcomes—their compilation by the American Council on Education and the American Association of Community and Junior Colleges is an important first step toward a more concise summary of what we know about community, technical, and junior colleges.

Daniel D. Savage
Vice President for Communication
   Services, American Association
   of Community and Junior Colleges

James C. Palmer
Director of Data Collection
   and Policy Analysis,
American Association of
   Community and Junior Colleges

I

General Information

Highlights: Profile Data

INSTITUTIONAL PROFILE

Number of Community Colleges

Public institutions	1088	(87 percent)
Independent institutions	154	(13 percent)
Total	1222	

Enrollment

Public institutions	4,703,000
Independent institutions	145,500
Total	4,848,500

Total Degrees Conferred:
454,712

Number of Faculty

Full-time faculty	110,909
Part-time faculty	164,080
Total faculty	274,989

Average Faculty Salary

Institutions with ranked faculty	$30,000
Unranked faculty	$31,240

Revenues

Appropriations

Local	$1.8 billion
State	$5.2 billion
Federal	$80 million

Grants/Contracts

	$58 million
	$255 million
	$1.3 billion

Expenditures

	Public Institutions	Independent Institutions
Current fund expenditures	$10.3 billion	$910 million
Current-fund expenditures per full-time equivalent student	$4,209	$4,433

Sources of Revenues

Local funds	23.4 percent
State funds	48.9 percent
Federal funds	7.4 percent
Tuition	17.4 percent

PROFILE OF STUDENTS IN COMMUNITY COLLEGES

Students by Age

14–21	46.7 percent
22–34	38.6 percent
35+	14.7 percent

Sex of Students

Women	2,590,000	56.0 percent
Men	2,040,000	44.0 percent

Attendance Status of Students

Full-time	1,730,000	63.0 percent
Part-time	2,900,000	37.0 percent

First-Time Freshmen

Total enrolled in higher education	2.3 million
Two-year public colleges	46.2 percent
Two-year independent colleges	5.1 percent

First-Time Freshmen by Sex

Women	56.6 percent
Men	45.4 percent

Transfer Rates

(Percentage of Two-Year Graduates Who Enter Four-Year Programs)

Public community colleges	42.1 percent
Public technical colleges	15.0 percent
Independent colleges	40.3 percent

Most Popular Fields for Associate Degrees

Business	26.6 percent
Liberal/general studies	23.4 percent
Health	15.1 percent
Engineering technologies	13.2 percent

PROFILE ON MINORITIES

Minority Enrollment in Two-Year Institutions

Hispanic	288,000
American Indian	45,000
Asian	165,000
Black	457,000

College Participation Rates for High-School Graduates, October 1980

Public Two-Year Colleges

Hispanic	20.3 percent
American Indian	18.5 percent
Asian	21.6 percent
Black	11.1 percent
Nonresident	16.5 percent

College Enrollment Rates of 18–24-Year-Old High-School Graduates

Total	33.7 percent
Hispanic	26.9 percent
Black	26.1 percent
White	34.4 percent

Persistence Rates in Two-Year Institutions

Percentage of Freshmen Who Were Enrolled 1½ Years Later

Total	59.0 percent
Hispanic	65.0 percent
American Indian	61.0 percent
Asian	70.0 percent
Black	61.0 percent
White	57.0 percent

High-School Completion Rates for 18–24-Year-Olds

Total	77.9 percent
Hispanic	54.2 percent
Black	71.3 percent
White	79.1 percent

High-School Completion Rates for Age 25 and Older

	1970	1985
Black	31.4 percent	59.8 percent
White	54.5 percent	75.5 percent
Hispanic	32.1 percent	47.9 percent

High-School Dropout Rates

	1970	1985
Total	17.0 percent	12.0 percent
Hispanic	33.0 percent	31.4 percent
Black	30.0 percent	15.5 percent
White	15.2 percent	11.5 percent

Educational Attainment among 25–29-Year-Olds

	1–3 Years of College	4 or More Years of College
Total	21.6 percent	22.2 percent
Black	22.9 percent	11.5 percent
Hispanic	15.9 percent	11.0 percent

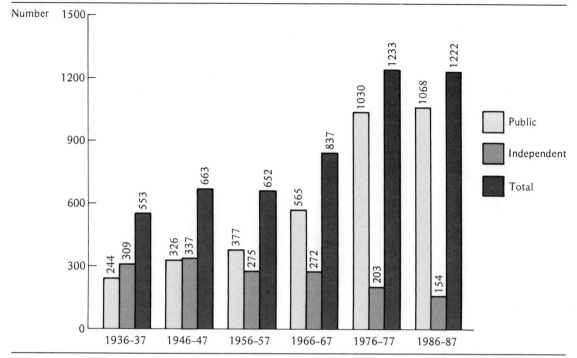

The number of community, technical, and junior colleges has grown tremendously in the last 50 years. Between 1936–37 and 1986–87, the number of two-year colleges more than doubled, from 553 to 1,222.

The largest growth period was between 1966–67 and 1976–77, with an increase of 47 percent during that period.

While the two-year segment has grown annually, the greatest growth has been in the public sector. The number of public two-year institutions increased four times between 1936–37 and 1986–87, while the number of independent colleges decreased 50 percent. In 1986–87, of the 1,222 two-year colleges, 87 percent were public and 13 percent were independent.

Source: AACJC, *Supplement to the AACJC Letter,* no. 234, March 24, 1987, p. 1.

2 Enrollment in Community, Technical, and Junior Colleges: 1936–37 to 1986–87

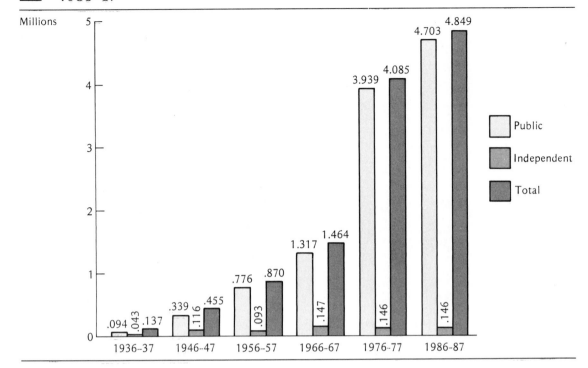

Between 1936–37 and 1986–87 enrollments in community, technical, and junior colleges increased over 35 times.[1]

Enrollment in these colleges made the greatest numerical gain between 1966–67 and 1976–77.[2]

Enrollments continued to increase during the last 10 years but at a slower rate—18.7 percent compared to 179.1 percent for the previous decade.

In academic year 1987, there were 32 times as many students enrolled in publicly controlled community, technical, and junior colleges as in independent two-year colleges.

Enrollment in independent two-year colleges peaked at 147,119 in 1966–67. Since that time, enrollment in independent two-year colleges has decreased by 1 percent to 145,500 in 1986–87.

Notes: 1. These figures will differ from data from the U.S. Census Bureau and the Center for Education Statistics because of differences in survey methodology.
2. Some of the increase shown in this table may be due to changing enrollment definitions during this period.

Source: AACJC, *Supplement to the AACJC Letter*, no. 234, March 24, 1987, p. 1.

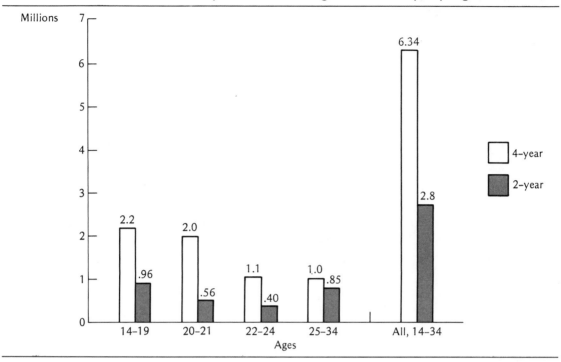

In 1985, 11 percent of all persons between the ages of 14–34 were enrolled for undergraduate study. Three percent, or 2.8 million, of these individuals were enrolled in two-year institutions.

Thirty-two percent of 20–21-year-olds were participating in undergraduate study. Of this number, 7 percent were attending two-year colleges. Participation rates for both undergraduate study and two-year colleges were largest for this age group.

The participation rate for 22–24-year-olds in undergraduate study was 12 percent. Similarly, 3 percent of 22–24-year-olds were attending two-year institutions.

Note: These figures will differ from figures from AACJC because of the use of different survey procedures: An institutional survey was used by AACJC for enrollment data and a household survey was used by the U.S. Census Bureau.

Source: *Current Population Reports,* P-20, no. 409, table 5, p. 7.

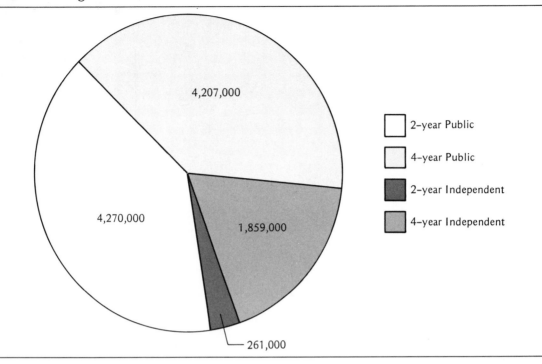

4,207,000

4,270,000

1,859,000

261,000

- ☐ 2–year Public
- ☐ 4–year Public
- ■ 2–year Independent
- ▧ 4–year Independent

In 1985, two-year colleges enrolled nearly 43 percent of the total undergraduate enrollment in higher education.

In Fall 1985, public two-year colleges enrolled a slightly higher percentage (40.3 percent) of all undergraduate students than did public four-year institutions (39.7 percent).

Independent colleges enrolled 20 percent of the 10.6 million undergraduate students in Fall 1985. Two-year independent schools enrolled approximately 3 percent of these students.

Note: These figures will differ from data from AACJC and the Census Bureau because of differences in survey methodology.

Sources: *Digest of Education Statistics, 1987,* tables 102, 109, 111, and 112, pp. 122, 129, and 131; Appendix Table A-1.

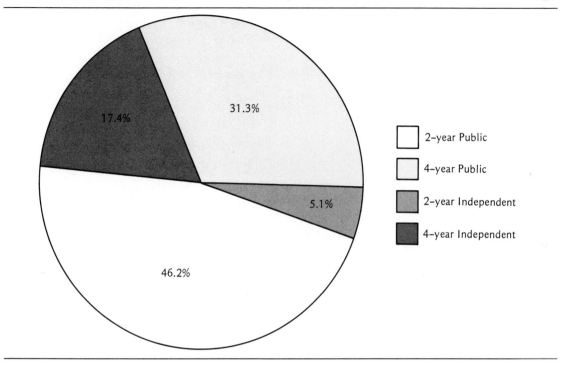

31.3%

17.4%

5.1%

46.2%

☐ 2–year Public

◻ 4–year Public

▨ 2–year Independent

▨ 4–year Independent

Of the 2.3 million first-time freshmen enrolled in higher education in Fall 1985, 51 percent were enrolled in two-year institutions and 49 percent were enrolled in four-year institutions.

In 1985, public two-year institutions enrolled the largest percentage of first-time freshmen (46 percent). First-time freshmen enrollment in two-year independent institutions represented another 5 percent of the total first-time freshman enrollment.

Source: *Digest of Education Statistics, 1987,* table 110, p. 130; Appendix Table A-1.

6 First-Time College Freshmen Enrollment in Two-Year Institutions, by Attendance Status and Sex: 1985

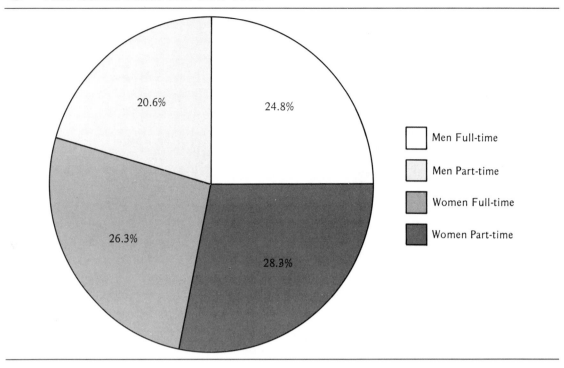

Men Full-time

Men Part-time

Women Full-time

Women Part-time

As of Fall 1985, full-time freshmen who enrolled in two-year colleges for the first time slightly outnumbered their part-time counterparts (591,443 compared to 574,691).

Among first-time freshmen, more women than men (54.6 percent versus 45.4 percent) enrolled in two-year institutions in Fall 1985.

Men who attended full-time comprised 24.8 percent of the first-time freshmen enrollment in two-year institutions, while women who attended full-time made up 26.3 percent of this enrollment.

Men who attended part-time accounted for the smallest percentage of the first-time freshmen enrollment (20.6 percent), and women who attended part-time comprised the largest percentage (28.3 percent).

Source: CES, unpublished tabulations.

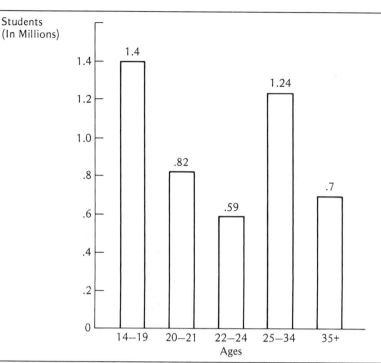

Students
(In Millions)

In 1985, nearly 30 percent (1.4 million) of the 4.7 million students enrolling in two-year colleges were age 19 and under.

According to estimates by the American Association of Community and Junior Colleges, 41 percent, or 1.9 million, of the students enrolled in community, technical, and junior colleges in Fall 1985 were 25 years of age and older. Approximately 15 percent, or 697,000, of these students were 35 years of age or older.

Students between the ages of 20–21 numbered nearly 815,000, or 17 percent of the total enrollment, while 22–24-year-olds accounted only for 12 percent, or 589,000, of the enrollment in community, technical, and junior colleges.

Note: These are estimates based upon the proportion of adults in the U.S. population who say they attend two-year colleges (see census data). The proportions for different age groups were applied to the total number of two-year college students enrolled in Fall 1985 as determined by the U.S. Department of Education. The enrollment data reported here differ from the enrollment data reported by the U.S. Census Bureau: the former are based on a survey of the colleges; the latter are based on self-reported data from U.S. households.

Source: AACJC, estimates calculated from *Current Population Reports* P-20, no. 409, table 5, p. 7; *Digest of Education Statistics, 1987* table 103, p. 123; Appendix Table A-2.

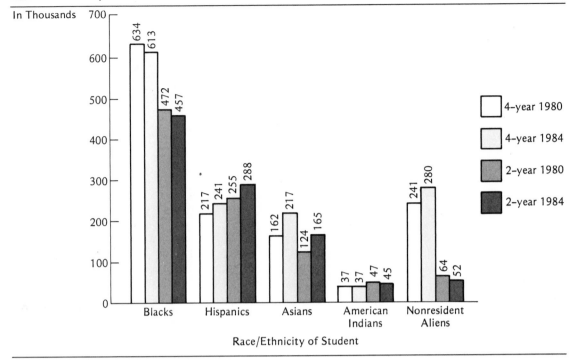

In Thousands

4-year 1980
4-year 1984
2-year 1980
2-year 1984

Race/Ethnicity of Student

In Fall 1984, 955,000 minority students attended two-year institutions.

Minorities are more likely to attend two-year colleges than whites or nonresident aliens. In Fall 1984, only 36 percent of the whites who enrolled in college and 16 percent of the nonresident aliens attended two-year colleges.

Of the 529,000 Hispanics enrolled in higher education, 54 percent were in two-year colleges in both Fall 1980 and Fall 1984.

Approximately 43 percent of the blacks and Asians who enrolled in college attended two-year institutions in 1984–85, compared to 54 percent of the American Indian college participants.

Source: *Digest of Education Statistics, 1987,* table 130, p. 151.

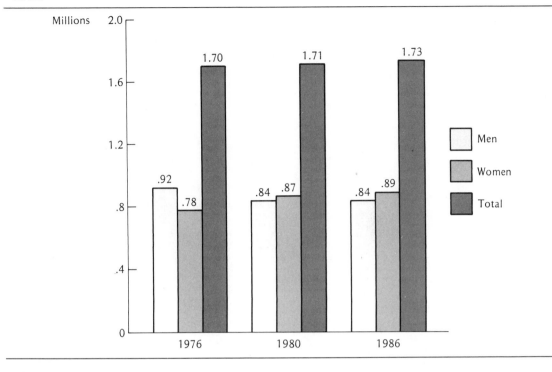

Between 1976 and 1980, full-time male enrollment in two-year institutions declined by 8 percent. Conversely, full-time female enrollment increased by 11 percent.

By 1986, the number of men enrolled full-time in two-year colleges made a slight gain, from 839,000 to 840,000. Full-time enrollment for women increased 2 percent between 1980 and 1986.

The increase in full-time female enrollment over the last decade offset the decline in full-time male enrollment.

Sources: CES, *Fall Enrollment in Higher Education,* 1976, table 7, p. 32; *Fall Enrollments in Colleges and Universities,* 1982, no. A, p. 98; unpublished tabulations from a Sample Survey of Estimates of Fall Enrollments, 1986.

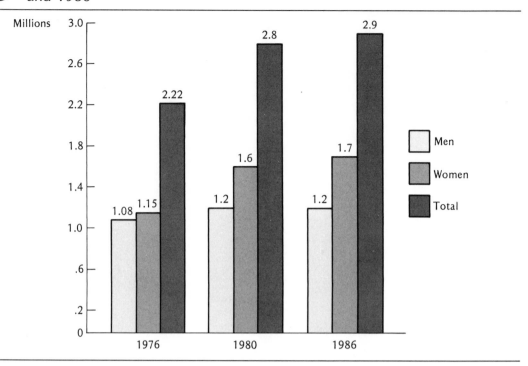

Two-year colleges have a significantly higher percentage of part-time students than do four-year institutions. In Fall 1986, 63 percent of the total enrollment in two-year institutions were enrolled part-time and 37 percent were enrolled full-time.

Between Fall 1976 and 1986 the part-time enrollment of women in two-year colleges increased 50 percent.

Between Fall 1976 and 1980 the part-time enrollment of men increased 11 percent. Since 1980 the part-time enrollment of men in two-year colleges has been relatively stable.

Sources: CES, *Fall Enrollments in Higher Education,* 1976, table 7, p. 32; *Fall Enrollments in Colleges and Universities,* 1982, table A, p. 98; unpublished tabulations from a Sample Survey of Estimates of Fall Enrollments, 1986.

Actual and Projected Part-Time and Full-Time Enrollment in Two-Year Institutions: 1970–1992

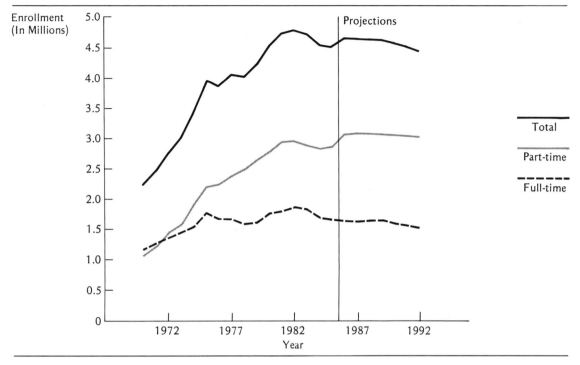

Between 1986 and 1992, the total enrollment in two-year institutions is estimated to decline 4 percent as a result of declines in full-time enrollment.

Full-time enrollment in two-year colleges is projected to decrease 10 percent by 1992 to 1.5 million, down from the 1985 level of 1.7 million students.

Note: The following projections were used because they were closest to the actual figures for prior years: total enrollment—low; full-time enrollment—intermediate; part-time enrollment—low.

Sources: CES, *Projections of Education Statistics to 1992–93,* table B-5B, p. 51; *Digest of Education Statistics, 1987,* table 107, p. 126.

12 Actual and Projected Full-Time-Equivalent Enrollment in Two-Year Institutions: 1970–1992

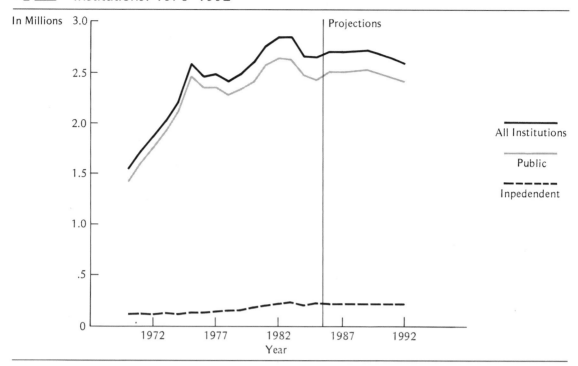

Full-time-equivalent (FTE) enrollment in two-year institutions is projected to decrease 4 percent between 1986 and 1992.

The projected decrease in FTE enrollment at two-year colleges will be caused by declines in FTE enrollment at public institutions during this period. A 4 percent decline is projected.

Between 1983 and 1985, the actual FTE enrollment in two-year institutions was higher than projected. According to estimates, FTE enrollment in independent two-year colleges will remain relatively constant between 1986 and 1992.

Note: The following projections were used since they were closest to the actual figures for prior years: total FTE—intermediate; public FTE—intermediate; independent FTE—high

Sources: CES, *Projections of Education Statistics to 1992–93,* tables B-13, B-13A and B-13B, pp. 65, 66, and 67; *Digest of Education Statistics, 1987,* no. 107, p. 126.

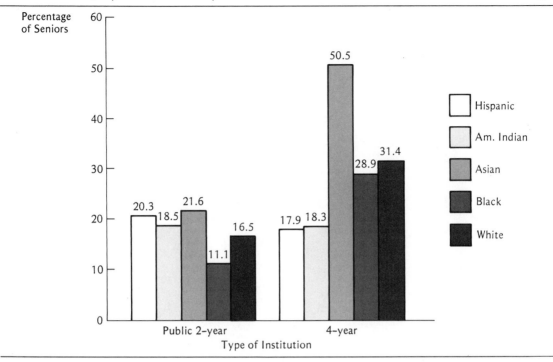

Approximately 38 percent of the Hispanic high-school seniors in 1980 entered college the following fall. Over half of these seniors attended a public two-year college. Of all ethnic groups, Hispanics had the highest concentration in two-year institutions.

American Indians had the lowest overall participation rate for high-school graduates entering higher education. Less than 37 percent entered college.

Of all racial/ethnic groups, Asians has the highest college enrollment rate for high-school graduates in Fall 1980. Over 72 percent of the Asian high-school seniors attended college directly after high school. The majority of Asian students who attended college attended four-year institutions. Only 22 percent attended public two-year institutions.

The college participation rate for black high-school graduates was 40 percent in Fall 1980. Eleven percent of all black high-school seniors attended two-year public colleges.

Note: Data were not available on two-year independent colleges in this follow-up study.
Source: CES, *Postsecondary Status and Persistence of the High School Graduates of 1980,* table 1, p. 1.

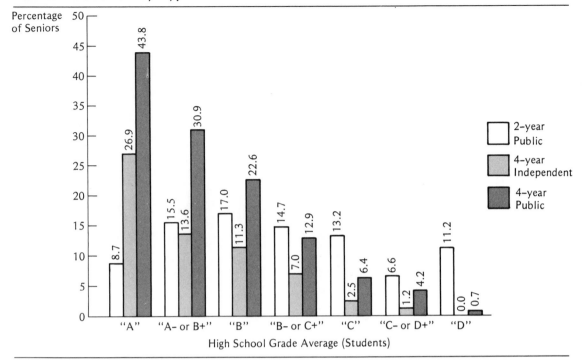

Percentage of Seniors

High School Grade Average (Students)

Legend:
- 2–year Public
- 4–year Independent
- 4–year Public

Values by grade average:

"A": 8.7, 26.9, 43.8
"A– or B+": 15.5, 13.6, 30.9
"B": 17.0, 11.3, 22.6
"B– or C+": 14.7, 7.0, 12.9
"C": 13.2, 2.5, 6.4
"C– or D+": 6.6, 1.2, 4.2
"D": 11.2, 0.0, 0.7

Only 9 percent of the high-school seniors who had an A average attended a two-year public college in 1980. Conversely, 44 percent of these same high-achieving students attended public four-year institutions, and 27 percent of them attended four-year independent institutions.

High-school seniors with an A– or B+ average attended public four-year colleges in a significantly higher proportion than they attended two-year institutions—31 percent compared to 16 percent.

Two-year colleges enrolled a higher percentage of high-school seniors with B and C averages than did four-year institutions. They also enrolled 11 percent of the high-school seniors with a D average. Four-year institutions enrolled less than 1 percent of the seniors with a D average.

Note: Data were not available on two-year independent colleges in this follow-up study.
Source: CES, unpublished tabulations from High School and Beyond: Second Follow-up Data, 1980 High School Seniors, July 1986, table 1, p. 1.

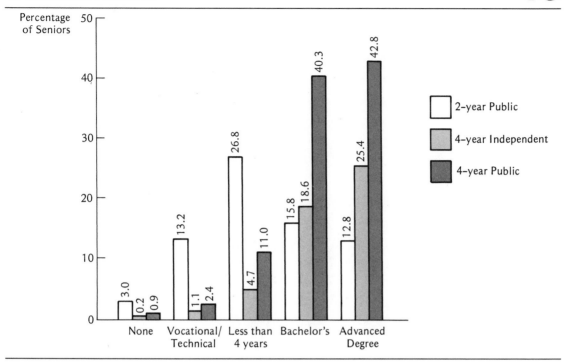

The postsecondary plans of high-school seniors who attended two-year institutions were considerably different from those entering four-year institutions (Fall 1980).

In Fall 1980, of the high-school seniors who planned to attend college for fewer than four years, approximately 27 percent entered a two-year public college, 11 percent entered a four-year public institution, and less than 5 percent entered an independent four-year institution.

In Fall 1980, 13 percent of the high-school seniors who planned to attend a vocational/technical school attended a public two-year college, while only 4 percent of these same students attended a four-year college.

High-school seniors who planned to obtain a baccalaureate degree were more likely to attend a four-year institution than a two-year public college (59 percent and 16 percent, respectively).

Only 13 percent of the students who planned to obtain an advanced degree attended a public two-year institution, while 69 percent attended a four-year college or university.

Note: Data were not available on two-year independent colleges in this follow-up study.
Source: CES, unpublished tabulations from High School and Beyond: Second Follow-up Data, 1980 High School Seniors, July 1986, table 1, p. 1.

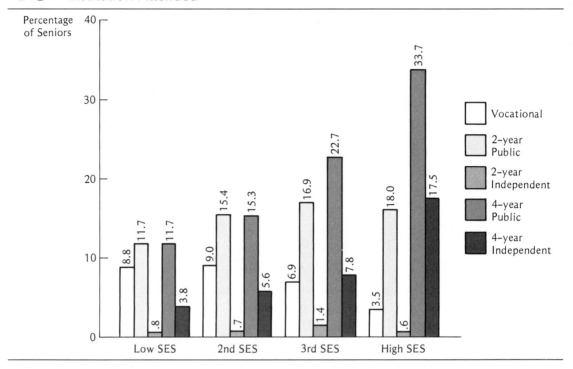

Socioeconomic status (SES), which combines family income and parental education, was a major determinant of whether 1980 high-school graduates attended a public or independent postsecondary institution.

In 1980, high-school seniors from low and low-middle SES attended public postsecondary institutions more frequently than they did independent institutions. Approximately 12 percent of low SES and 15 percent of low-middle SES seniors attended public two-year colleges. Approximately the same percentages attended public four-year institutions.

Seniors with high socioeconomic status were the least likely to attend a vocational school; less than 4 percent of these students attended this type of postsecondary school.

In 1980, approximately 17 percent of upper-middle SES and 16 percent of the upper SES seniors attended a public junior, technical, or community college, compared to the 23 percent and 34 percent who attended public four-year colleges or universities.

Sources: CES, *High School and Beyond: Transition from High School to Postsecondary Education*, Feb. 1987, table 4–1, p. 78.

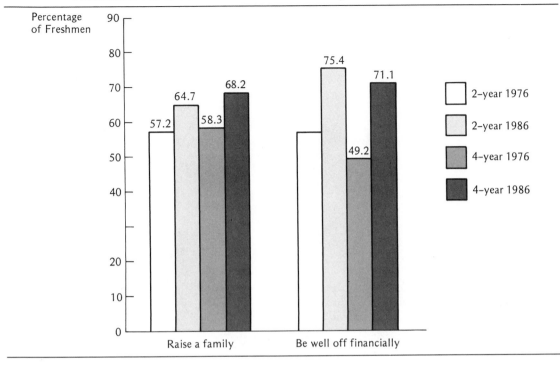

The importance of being "very well off financially" gained dramatically as a significant value for both two-year and four-year first-time freshmen between 1976 and 1986.

- In 1976, 57 percent of the two-year college freshmen considered this value "very important," compared to 75 percent of the 1986 two-year college freshmen.
- A similar increase occurred in the percentage of four-year college freshmen who considered this value "very important"—49 percent in 1976, compared to 71 percent in 1986.

In 1986, more first-time college freshmen considered it important to raise a family than in 1976.

- In 1976, 57 percent of the freshmen at two-year colleges considered this value "very important," compared to 65 percent in 1986.
- Approximately 58 percent of the freshmen at four-year colleges thought raising a family was essential, compared to 68 percent in 1986.

Note: Data are from studies of characteristics of students entering college as first-time, full-time freshmen.

Source: Astin et al., *The American Freshman,* Fall 1976, p. 60, and Fall 1986, p. 64; Appendix Tables A-4 and A-5.

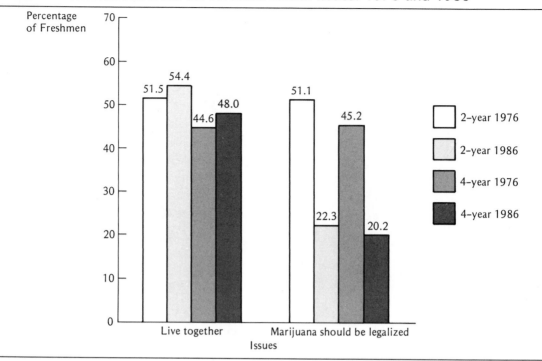

The percentage of college freshmen who thought it was acceptable to live together before marriage increased slightly between 1976 and 1986.

In 1986, a higher percentage of the freshmen enrolled in two-year colleges (54 percent) agreed with the concept of living together before marriage than their counterparts in four-year colleges (48 percent).

A significantly smaller percentage of the 1986 college freshmen agreed that marijuana should be legalized than in 1976.

- Approximately 51 percent of the 1976 two-year freshmen and 45 percent of the four-year freshmen agreed with legalization of marijuana.
- In 1986, these figures dropped to 22 percent of the two-year college freshmen and 20 percent of the four-year college freshmen.

Note: Data are from studies of characteristics of students entering college as first-time, full-time freshmen.

Source: Astin et al., *The American Freshman*, Fall 1976, p. 55, and Fall 1986, p. 64; Appendix Tables A-4 and A-5.

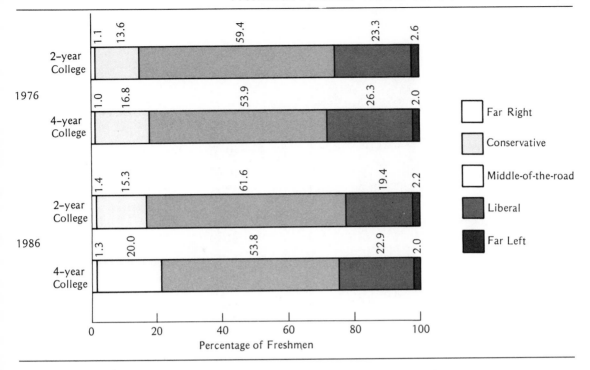

In Fall 1986, a slightly higher percentage of both two-year and four-year first-time college freshmen considered their political views either middle-of-the-road or conservative than their counterparts did in 1976. The percentage of students with liberal political views decreased 4 percent both in two-year and four-year colleges.

In Fall 1986, the majority (62 percent) of two-year-college freshmen considered their political views middle-of-the-road, while 54 percent of the four-year-college freshmen reported such a political orientation.

Approximately 19 percent of the two-year-college freshmen considered their views liberal, compared to 23 percent of their four-year-college counterparts (Fall 1986).

Fifteen percent of the freshmen who attended two-year colleges in Fall 1986 considered their political views conservative, compared to 20 percent of those who attended four-year institutions.

Note: Data are from studies of characteristics of students entering college as first-time, full-time freshmen.

Source: Astin et al., *The American Freshman,* Fall 1976, p. 45, and Fall 1986, p. 64; Appendix Tables A-4 and A-5.

20 Percentage of Graduates of Two-Year Programs Who Entered Four-Year Programs: 1980 and 1985

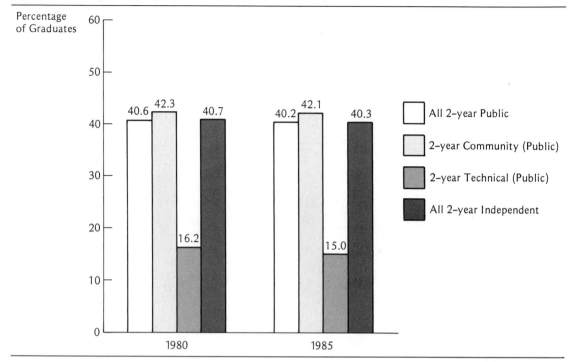

Forty percent of the students who completed their two-year degrees at a two-year college entered a four-year institution (1985).

Between 1980 and 1985, the number of students who completed a degree at a two-year college and entered a four-year institution remained relatively constant.

In 1985, the transfer rate to four-year degree programs was estimated to be 42 percent for community colleges and 15 percent for technical colleges.

During that same year, the transfer rate for public community colleges was slightly higher (42 percent) than for independent colleges (40 percent).

Source: College Board, *Annual Survey of Colleges, 1986–87 Summary Statistics,* table 43, p. 90; General Information Surveys, U.S. Department of Education, 1984; Appendix Tables A-9 and A-10.

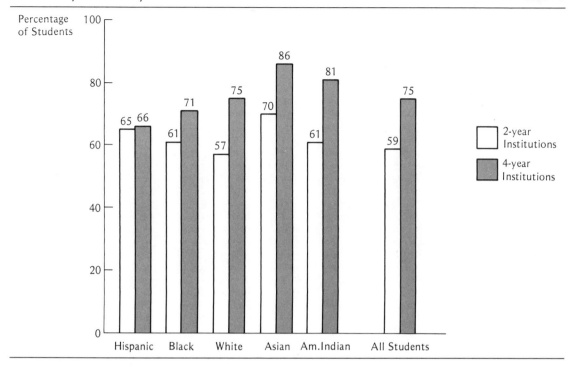

Of the high-school seniors who entered a two-year college, 59 percent were still enrolled
1½ years later. The persistence figure for their counterparts in a four-year college was
75 percent.

Race/ethnicity affects the college persistence rate of high-school seniors as follows:

- Asians had the highest persistence rate after 1½ years both in four-year and two-year colleges—86 percent and 70 percent, respectively.
- Whites had a low persistence rate in two-year institutions (57 percent), compared to a persistence rate of 75 percent in four-year institutions.
- The persistence rate for Hispanics was above average in two-year colleges (65 percent) and below average in four-year institutions (66 percent).
- Blacks were slightly above the average persistence rate in two-year colleges (61 percent) and below the average in four-year colleges (71 percent).

Note: Students who completed short-term programs and/or transferred to another institution were not included in these estimates of students who persisted in college.

Source: CES, *High School and Beyond, Two Years After High School: A Capsule Description of 1980 Seniors,* table 4, p. 9; Appendix Table A-7.

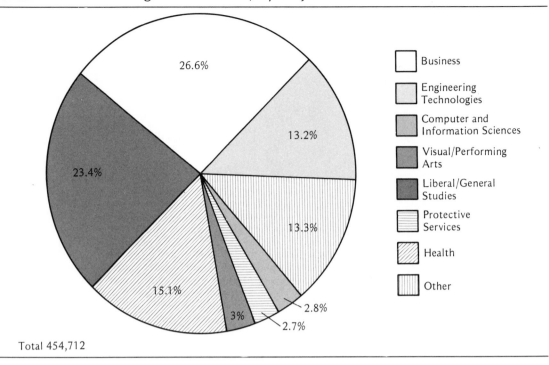

Business

Engineering
Technologies

Computer and
Information Sciences

Visual/Performing
Arts

Liberal/General
Studies

Protective
Services

Health

Other

Total 454,712

The number of associate degrees awarded between 1983 and 1985 remained relatively stable. There was a slight decline (less than 1 percent) in the total associate degrees awarded during this period.

Between 1983 and 1985, men received 2 percent fewer associate degrees, while women gained 1 percent in the number of degrees awarded.

In 1985, the largest number of associate degrees were awarded in business and management. The number of associate degrees awarded in this area (120,731) has been relatively constant since 1983. In 1985, over a quarter of associate-degree recipients were in this field of study.

Approximately 3 percent fewer associate degrees were awarded in liberal/general studies in 1985 than in 1983. This was the second largest degree area.

Degrees awarded in the health sciences increased 3 percent, from 66,448 in 1983 to 68,453 in 1985. The heaviest concentration of degrees in this area was in general nursing.

Engineering technologies was the fourth largest field of concentration, with 58,898 students receiving degrees in 1983 and 59,951 in 1985 (a 2 percent increase).

Source: CES, unpublished tabulations from Associate Degrees and Other Awards Below the Baccalaureate, 1983 to 1985, table 1.1, p. 35; Appendix Table A-8.

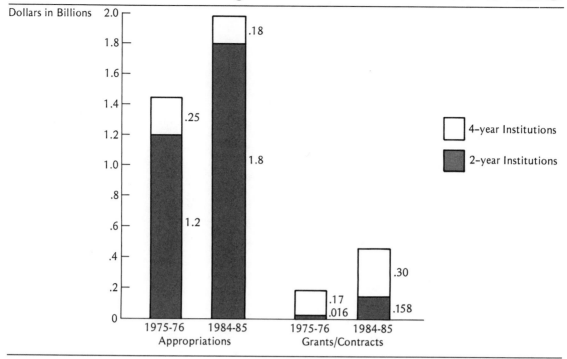

Between 1975–76 and 1984–85, local funding to higher education[1] increased 50 percent. These funds totaled $2.4 billion dollars in 1984–85. Of that total, approximately $2 billion came from local government appropriations.

Two-year institutions[2] received 91 percent of the local appropriations for higher education in 1984–85, compared to 82 percent in 1975–76.

In 1984–85, two-year institutions received 16 percent of the $357 million in local grants and contracts ($58 million).

Notes: 1. Includes outlying areas.

2. Two-year programs located on four-year campuses are included under two-year institutions.

Source: ACE, Division of Policy Analysis and Research tabulations based on Higher Education General Information Surveys, U.S. Department of Education, 1984; Appendix Tables A-9 and A-10.

24 State Revenues to Higher Education: 1975–76 and 1984–85

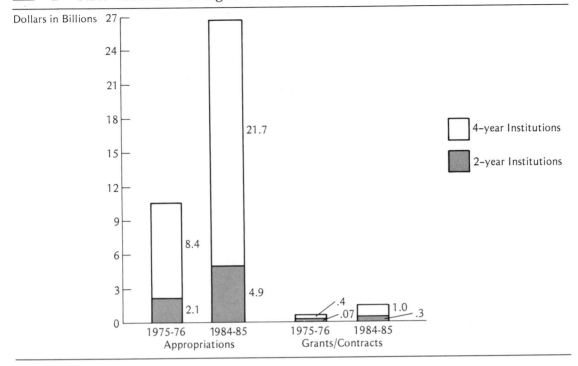

Two-year colleges received 19 percent of the state funding to higher education in 1975–76 and in 1984–85.

- In 1975–76, they received $2.1 billion. By 1984–85, this figure increased to $5.2 billion.
- Four-year colleges and universities were awarded $8.9 billion during the earlier period and $22.6 billion in 1984–85.

In 1984–85, two-year colleges received 23 percent of restricted grants and contracts awarded by the states, compared to 15 percent in 1975–76 ($255 million and $61 million, respectively).

Notes: 1. Two-year branches of four-year institutions are included under two-year institutions.

2. Includes outlying areas.

Source: ACE, Division of Policy Analysis and Research tabulations based on Higher Education General Information surveys, U.S. Department of Education, 1984; Appendix Tables A-9 and A-10.

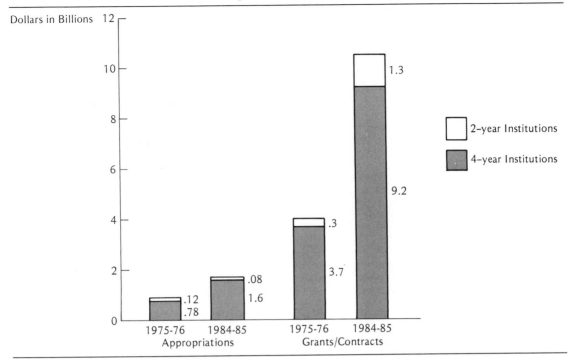

Dollars in Billions

2-year Institutions

4-year Institutions

In 1975–76, two-year institutions[1] were allocated $420 million, which was approximately 8 percent of total federal dollars to higher education[2]; by 1984–85, their share had increased to $1.4 billion, which represented 10 percent of the $12 billion funded to higher education.

The percentage of federal appropriations received by two-year institutions has decreased during this period, while their share of federal grants increased.

- Two-year colleges received 13 percent of the federal appropriations in 1975–76 and 5 percent in 1984–85.
- Grants to two-year institutions were 7 percent in 1975–76 and 11 percent in 1984–85.

Notes: 1. Two-year programs located on four-year campuses are included under two-year institutions.
2. Includes outlying areas.

Source: ACE, Department of Policy Analysis and Research tabulations based on Higher Education General Information surveys, U.S. Department of Education, 1984; Appendix Tables A-9 and A-10.

Changes in Percentage Distribution of Revenues to Two-Year Institutions: 1985 and 1986

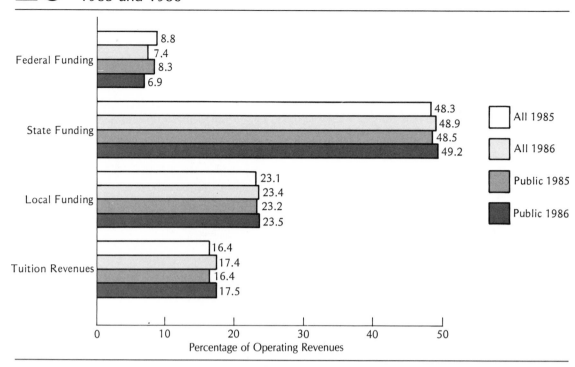

Percentage of Operating Revenues

According to estimates from the American Association of Community and Junior Colleges, federal support for public community, technical, and junior colleges dropped nearly 17 percent between Fall 1985 and Fall 1986.

During that same period, both state and local funds to these institutions remained relatively constant.

Declines in federal support were made up in part by increases in tuition revenues. In Fall 1985, tuition accounted for 16 percent of the average community college's income, and by 1986 this figure increased to 17.5 percent, yielding an increase of nearly 7 percent in tuition costs.

Source: AACJC, *Supplement to the AACJC Letter,* no. 245, June 16, 1987; Appendix Table A-12.

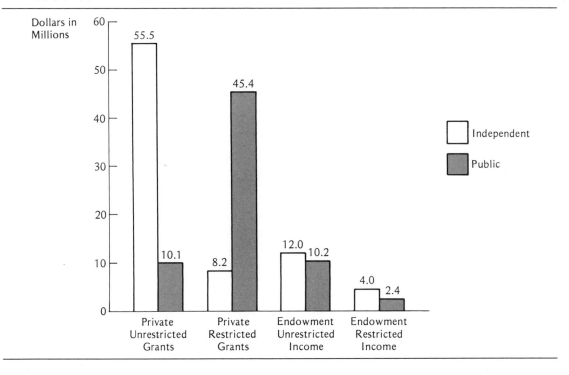

In 1984–85, income from private gifts and endowments accounted for only 1 percent of the total revenues of two-year institutions.

Of the $119.2 million in private gifts, grants, and contracts received by two-year colleges, $55.5 million went to public institutions and $63.7 million went to independent institutions.

Public institutions received 85 percent of the restricted private gifts awarded to two-year colleges ($45.4 million). Independent institutions received $55.5 million in unrestricted private gifts, which totaled 35 percent of this funding category.

Endowment income to two-year colleges was divided as follows:

Unrestricted	Restricted
Independent—56 percent	Independent—63 percent
Public—44 percent	Public—37 percent

Notes: 1. Two-year branches of four-year institutions are included under two-year institutions.

2. Includes outlying areas.

Source: ACE, Division of Policy Analysis and Research tabulations based on Higher Education General Information surveys, U.S. Department of Education, 1984; Appendix Tables A-9 and A-10.

28 Current-Fund Expenditures per FTE Student in Constant 1984–85 Dollars, by Type and Control

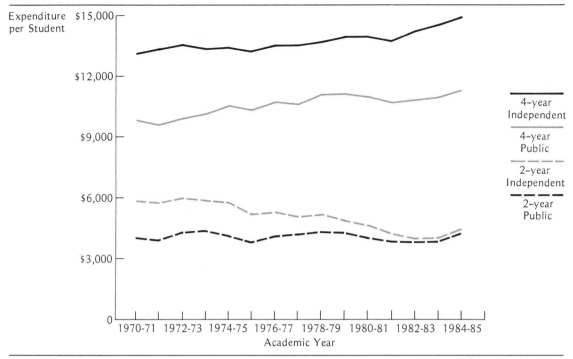

After adjustment for inflation, the current-fund expenditures per full-time-equivalent (FTE) student in two-year institutions increased from $4,139 in 1970–71 to $4,219 in 1984–85, or 1.9 percent in constant 1984–85 dollars. Expenditures per FTE student in independent two-year institutions decreased 25 percent between 1970–71 and 1984–85, from $5,883 to $4,433. Independent two-year colleges were the only institutions that experienced a decrease in expenditures per FTE; public two-year colleges increased FTE spending by 4.8 percent, from $4,009 to $4,201.

While expenditures per FTE student increased only slightly in two-year institutions, expenditures per FTE student increased 15 percent in all four-year institutions, from $10,890 in 1970–71 to $12,516 by 1984–85. There was a 14 percent increase at independent four-year institutions and a 15 percent increase at public four-year institutions.

Source: *Digest of Education Statistics, 1987,* table 205, p. 235; Appendix Table A-13.

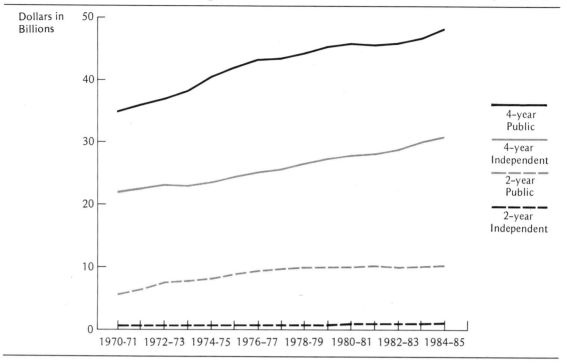

Dollars in Billions (y-axis: 0, 10, 20, 30, 40, 50)

Legend:
4-year Public
4-year Independent
2-year Public
2-year Independent

x-axis: 1970-71 1972-73 1974-75 1976-77 1978-79 1980-81 1982-83 1984-85

Trend data show increases in expenditures for both two-year and four-year institutions. After adjusting for inflation, current fund expenditures increased 78 percent for two-year institutions and 28 percent for four-year institutions between 1970–71 and 1984–85.

Spending increased 48 percent at two-year institutions between 1970–71 and 1974–75 and 12 percent between 1975–76 and 1984–85.

Between 1975–76 and 1984–85, independent two-year colleges increased spending by 55 percent, while public two-year colleges experienced a 10 percent increase in spending.

The increases in expenditures are almost entirely accounted for by increases in enrollment. Per-student expenditures increased only 1 percent in the 15-year period.

Note: Dollars adjusted by the higher education price index.
Source: *Digest of Education Statistics, 1987,* no. 205, p. 235; Appendix Table A-13.

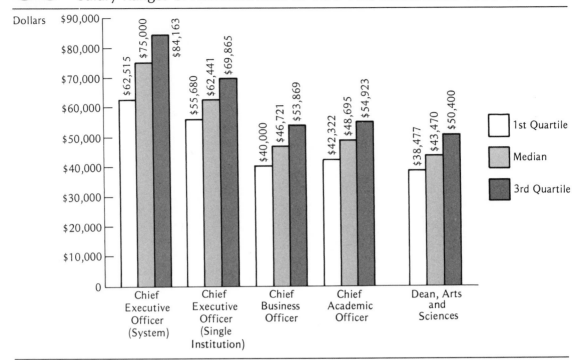

The median salary of a president of a two-year college was $62,400 in 1986–87, compared to $75,000 for the president of a system of two-year colleges.

In 1986–87, the median salaries for the following positions at two-year colleges were:

- Chief Academic Officer $48,695
- Chief Business Officer $46,721
- Dean, Arts and Sciences $43,470

Salaries of key administrative officers at public two-year institutions are 20–40 percent higher than those at independent two-year institutions.

Source: CUPA, *Administrative Compensation Survey,* 1986–87, table 19, p. 19. Appendix Table A-14.

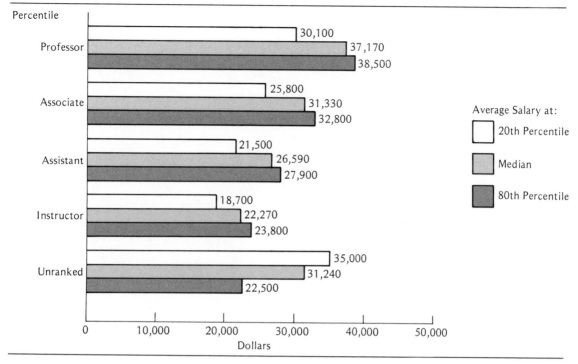

The average salary for all faculty at two-year colleges that ranked faculty was $30,100, compared to $31,240 at two-year colleges that did not rank their faculty.

Full professors in two-year colleges that ranked faculty had an average salary of $37,170 in 1986–87; associate professors received an average salary of $31,330; assistant professors received $26,590; and instructors received $22,270.

In 1986–87, salaries for unranked faculty at two-year institutions ranged from $40,500 to $22,500.

Source: AAUP, *Academe*, March–April 1987, table 3 and 6; Appendix Tables A-15 and A-16.

32 Full-Time and Part-Time Faculty at Community, Junior, and Technical Colleges: 1976–1986

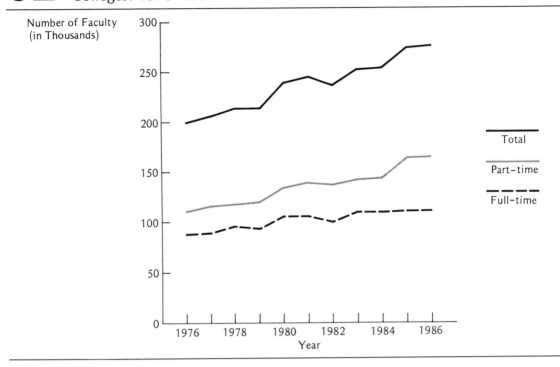

Number of Faculty (in Thousands)

Total
Part-time
Full-time

Year

There was a 38 percent increase in the number of faculty in community, technical, and junior colleges between 1976 and 1986. Total faculty numbers increased from 199,691 in 1976 to 274,989 in 1986.

Part-time faculty grew at a significantly faster pace than full-time faculty. Part-time faculty increased from 111,378 to 164,080, a net gain of 47 percent. Full-time faculty increased 26 percent, from 88,277 in 1976 to 110,909 by 1986.

The number of two-year college faculty increased at a fairly steady rate throughout this period. A decrease in the number of faculty in 1984 may have been caused by underreporting for this year.

Note: Beginning in 1985, staffing data are weighted by enrollment to adjust unreported staff totals. Prior to 1985, faculty data were usually compiled for all colleges, while data for professional support and administrative staff were underreported.

Source: AACJC, *Annual Survey of Colleges,* 1976–1986; Appendix Table A-17.

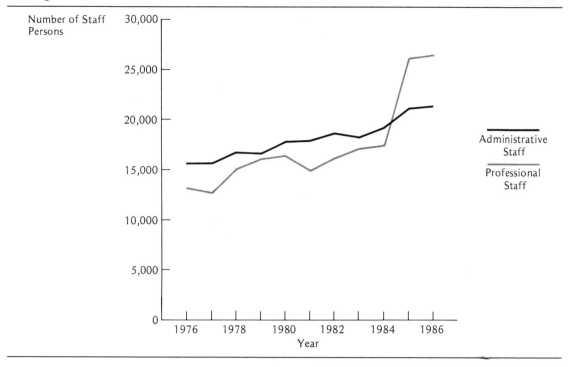

Number of Staff Persons

Administrative Staff

Professional Staff

Year

Between 1976 and 1986, the number of administrative staff in community, technical, and junior colleges increased 36 percent, from 15,653 to 21,370.

During the same period, professional support staff doubled, from 13,180 to 26,397.

Note: Beginning in 1985, staffing data are weighted by enrollment to adjust unreported staff totals. Prior to 1985, faculty data were usually compiled for all colleges, while data for professional support and administrative staff were underreported.

Source: AACJC, *Annual Survey of Colleges*, 1976–1986; Appendix Table A-17.

II

Planning Information for Community Colleges

Demographic and Economic Data Highlights

POPULATION

U.S. Population

(Total including armed forces overseas)	243,571,000
Resident population	243,050,000

Regional Distribution of U.S. Population

Northeast	20.9 percent
Midwest	24.8 percent
South	34.3 percent
West	20.0 percent

Regions with the most growth
1980–1985: South and West

Projected Population Increases (1985–2000)

Total	14.1 percent
Hispanic	49.1 percent
Black	27.0 percent
White	11.5 percent

Projected Changes in the Number of High School Graduates

1987–1989	4.0 percent increase
1990–1995	7.6 percent decrease

Projected Decreases in the 18–34 Years-Old Population (1985–2030)

18–24 year-olds	8.7 percent
25–34 year-olds	11.0 percent

INCOME

Median Family Income

Hispanic	$19,027
Black	$16,786
White	$29,152

Median Income of Persons with 1–3 Years of College

Men	$21,378
Women	$8,583

EMPLOYMENT

U.S. Labor Force

Total employment	120 million
Civilian employment	118 million
Unemployment rate	6.9 percent

Fastest Growing Occupations (1986–2000) Projected Increases

Computer system analysts	76.0 percent
Computer programmer	70.0 percent
Electrical and electronics engineers	49.0 percent
Registered nurses	44.0 percent

34 Educational Attainment of the U.S. Population, Age 25 and Over: 1910–1985

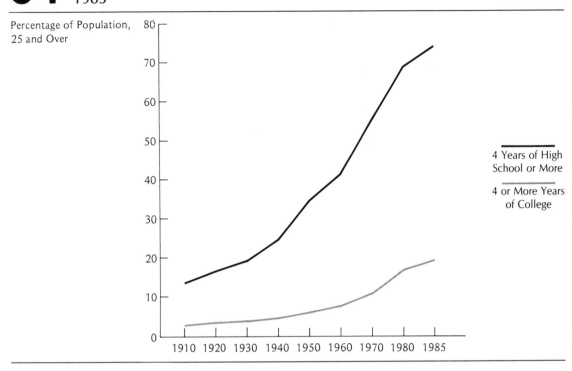

Percentage of Population, 25 and Over

4 Years of High School or More

4 or More Years of College

Educational levels of the U.S. population have increased dramatically since 1910.

- In 1910, only 13.5 percent of the population (age 25 and over) had completed four years of high-school education.
- In 1940, 24.5 percent of the population had this much schooling.
- By 1970, more than half of the population (55.2 percent) had four years of high-school education.

Between 1970 and 1985, the percentage of the population that completed at least four years of high school increased rapidly, rising to 62.5 percent by 1975, to 68.6 percent by 1980, and to 73.9 percent by 1985.

Source: *Digest of Education Statistics, 1987,* table 8, p. 13; Appendix Table A-18.

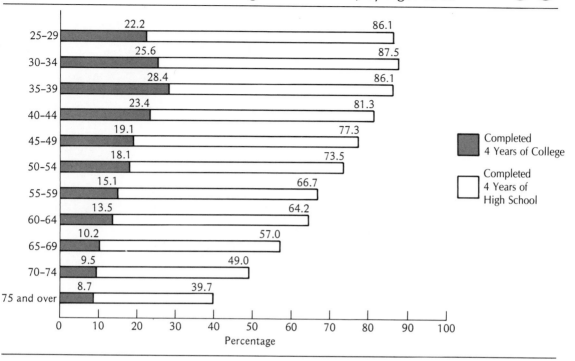

Older and younger Americans in 1985 had very different educational profiles.

- Among Americans 75 and older, 39.7 percent completed 4 years of high school.
- Among Americans 65–69 years of age, 57 percent completed 4 years of high school.
- Among Americans 55–59 years of age, two-thirds completed 4 years of high school.
- In contrast, among 30–34-year-olds, 87.5 percent had completed 4 years of high school.

Among Americans who are 25–29 years old, fewer than 4 percent had completed only 8 years of schooling.

Among Americans who are 55 and over, one in four (27.8 percent) had completed only 8 years of schooling.

Source: *Current Population Reports,* P-23, no. 150, p. 29.

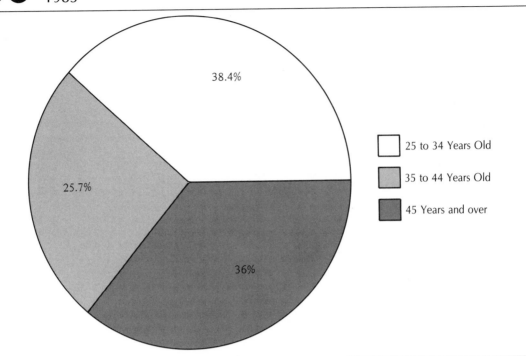

Legend:
- 25 to 34 Years Old
- 35 to 44 Years Old
- 45 Years and over

38.4%

25.7%

36%

In March 1985, 16.3 percent of the population (age 25 and over) had completed between 1 and 3 years of college. Another 19.4 percent had completed 4 years or more of college.

Of the 23.4 million Americans in 1985 who had completed at least 1 year but no more than 3 years of college, approximately 2.2 million were black and about 930,000 were of Hispanic origin.

Among Americans in this age group who have between 1 and 3 years of college, almost 4 in 10 (38.4 percent) are between 25 and 34 years of age. Two-thirds are under 45 years of age.

Note: Surveys by the U.S. Census Bureau do not identify persons who completed 2 years of college study.
Source: *Statistical Abstract, 1987*, table 199, p. 122; Appendix Table A-19.

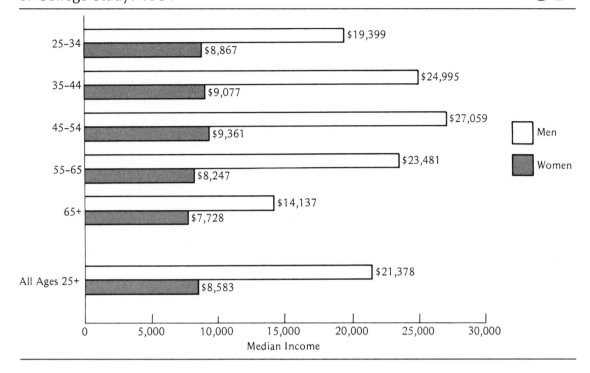

In 1984, the median income of all persons age 25 and over who had 1–3 years of college was estimated at $14,980. The figure for men ($21,373) was 2½ times that for women ($8,583).

The median income for women with this level of education did not vary greatly by age. Women in the age category 65+ were estimated to have the lowest median income, $7,728. Women in the 45–54 age bracket reported the highest median income, $9,361.

Age made a big difference for men. The lowest median income of men with this level of education was reported for the 65+ age bracket, $14,137. Men in the age bracket 45–54 reported the highest median income, $27,059.

More education makes a difference. The median income of all persons with 1–3 years of college was 14 percent higher than the median income of those who had only a high-school diploma. Those who had at least 4 years of college reported median incomes about 25 percent higher than those with 1–3 years of college.

Note: Surveys by the Census Bureau do not identify persons who completed 2 years of college study.

Source: *Digest of Education Statistics, 1987*, table 29, pp. 286–287.

38 Educational Attainment among 25–29-Year-Old Americans, by Race/Ethnicity: 1985

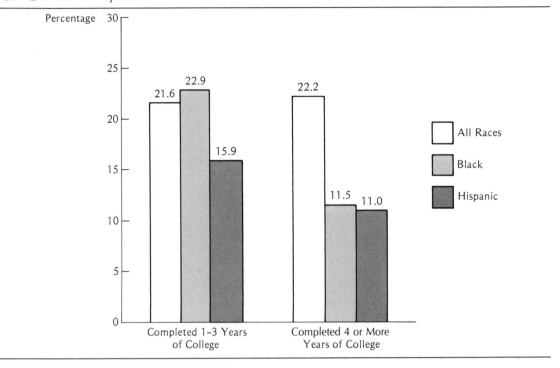

Americans between 25 and 29 years of age have completed significantly more education than other Americans.

In 1985, 43.8 percent of Americans between 25 and 29 years of age had completed some amount of postsecondary education. This figure included 21.6 percent who completed 1–3 years of college and another 22.2 percent who completed 4 years or more of college.

Among blacks between the ages of 25 and 29, 22.9 percent had completed between 1 and 3 years of college, and another 11.5 percent had completed 4 years or more of college study.

Among Hispanics between the ages of 25–29, 15.9 percent had completed between 1 and 3 years of college, and another 11.0 percent had completed 4 years or more of college study.

Source: *Statistical Abstract, 1987,* table 199, p. 122; Appendix Table A-19.

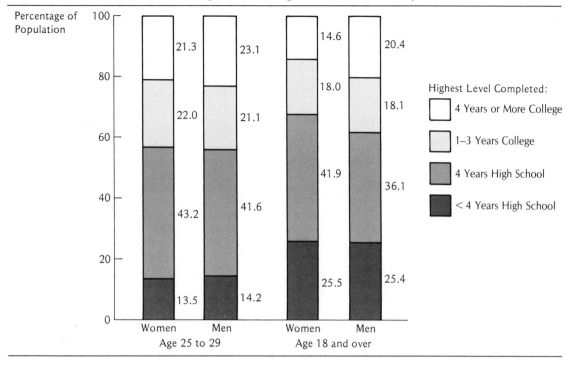

In 1985, 16.2 million women (age 18 and over) and 14.8 million men had completed 1–3 years of college.

Another 8.5 million women and 9.3 million men had completed 4 years of college, and 4.7 million women and 7.3 million men had completed 5 years or more of college.

In 1985, differences in educational attainment between American men and women (age 18 and over) appeared primarily at the postsecondary level. Among men, 38.5 percent had completed some amount of postsecondary education; among women, only 32.6 percent had done so.

The largest educational difference was in completion of 4 years or more of college. Among persons age 18 and over, 20.4 percent of men but only 14.6 percent of women had completed 4 years or more of college in 1985.

Among younger persons, between 25 and 29 years old, this gap has narrowed: 23.1 percent of men completed 4 years of college, compared to 21.3 percent of women.

Sources: *Statistical Abstract, 1987,* table 199, p. 122; *Digest of Education Statistics, 1987,* table 9, p. 14; Appendix Tables A-19 and A-20.

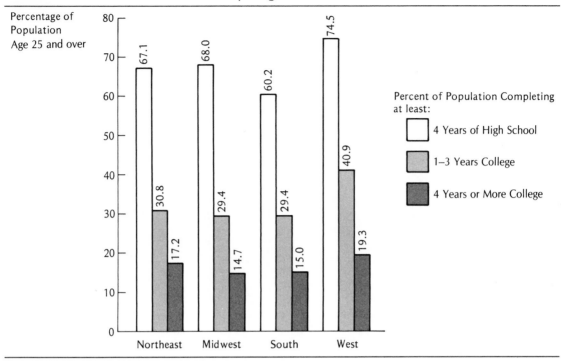

Percentage of Population Age 25 and over

67.1   68.0   60.2   74.5
30.8   29.4   29.4   40.9
17.2   14.7   15.0   19.3

Northeast   Midwest   South   West

Percent of Population Completing at least:

☐ 4 Years of High School

▨ 1–3 Years College

▮ 4 Years or More College

Levels of educational attainment in 1980 were higher in the West than in other U.S. regions.

The states having the highest percentage of the population with 1 year or more of college in 1980 included the following:

Utah	44.1	Washington	40.2
Colorado	44.1	Hawaii	38.8
Alaska	43.7	Oregon	38.5
California	42.0	Arizona	38.0
Dist. Columbia	41.5	Wyoming	37.9

The states having the lowest percentage of the population with 1 year or more of college included the following:

West Virginia	20.4	Indiana	24.6
Kentucky	21.8	Alabama	24.7
Arkansas	22.3	Mississippi	25.6
Pennsylvania	24.3	South Carolina	26.7
Tennessee	24.5	Louisiana	26.7

Source: *Statistical Abstract, 1986,* table 217, p. 134; Appendix Table A-21.

Persons Age 25 and Over Who Completed High School, by Race/Ethnicity: 1970, 1980, and 1985

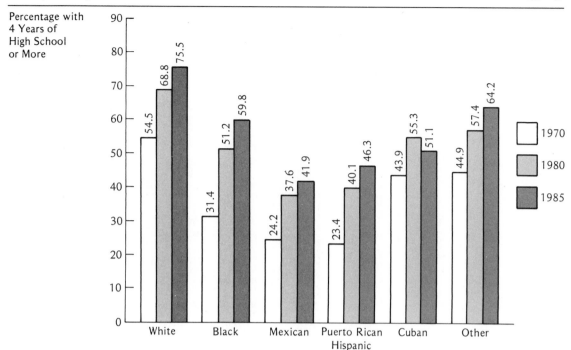

Percentage with 4 Years of High School or More

Legend: 1970, 1980, 1985

Categories: White, Black, Mexican, Puerto Rican, Cuban, Other — Hispanic

White: 54.5, 68.8, 75.5
Black: 31.4, 51.2, 59.8
Mexican: 24.2, 37.6, 41.9
Puerto Rican: 23.4, 40.1, 46.3
Cuban: 43.9, 55.3, 51.1
Other: 44.9, 57.4, 64.2

In 1985, three-fifths of black adults (59.8 percent) and fewer than half of Hispanics (47.9 percent) who were ages 25 and over had completed 4 years or more of high school.

The percentage of black adults with 4 years of high-school education has almost doubled since 1970 (31.4 percent in 1970, compared to 59.8 percent in 1985).

In 1985, 41.9 percent of Mexican American adults and 46.3 percent of Puerto Rican adults had completed 4 years of high school.

Seventeen percent of Mexican American adults and 12.8 percent of Puerto Rican adults have completed less than 5 years of schooling. For the entire U.S. population (age 25 and over), 2.7 percent have completed less than 5 years of schooling.

Source: *Statistical Abstract, 1987,* table 200, p. 122; Appendix Table A-22.

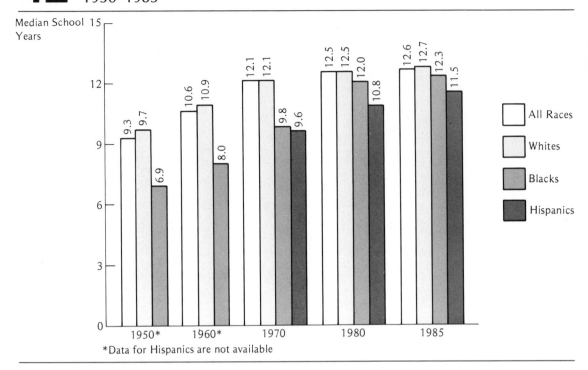

Median School Years

*Data for Hispanics are not available

Legend:
- All Races
- Whites
- Blacks
- Hispanics

Year	All Races	Whites	Blacks	Hispanics
1950*	9.3	9.7	6.9	
1960*	10.6	10.9	8.0	
1970	12.1	12.1	9.8	9.6
1980	12.5	12.5	12.0	10.8
1985	12.6	12.7	12.3	11.5

Educational levels of the black and Hispanic population (age 25 and over) were lower than for whites in 1985 but have shown improvement over the last 3 decades.

In 1985, the median years of school completed for blacks (age 25 and over) was 12.3 years, compared to 12.7 years for whites. For Hispanics, the median number of years completed was lower, 11.5 years.

In 1970, in contrast, the median years of school completed was 9.8 years for blacks and 9.6 years for Hispanics, compared to 12.1 years for whites.

In 1950, the median years of school completed for blacks was 6.9 years, compared to 9.7 years for whites.

In 1985, 59.8 percent of blacks and 47.9 percent of Hispanics (age 25 and over) had completed 4 years or more of high school; 14.8 percent of blacks and 11.0 percent of Hispanics had completed 1–3 years of college.

Source: *Statistical Abstract, 1987*, table 199, p. 122, and table 200, p. 122; *Statistical Abstract, 1986*, no. 215, p. 133; Appendix Tables A-21 and A-22.

High-School Graduates, Age 18–24, Enrolled in College, by Race/Ethnicity: 1976, 1980, and 1985

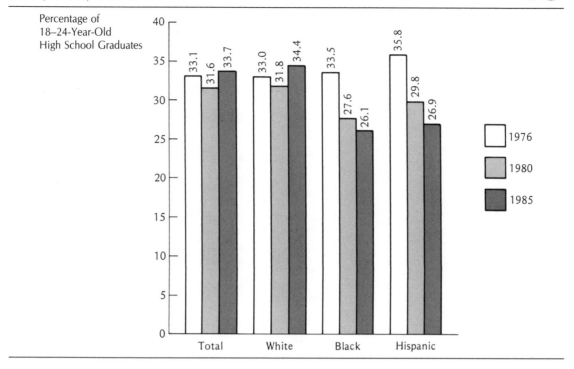

Percentage of 18–24-Year-Old High School Graduates

	1976
	1980
	1985

About one-third of high-school graduates between the ages of 18–24 were enrolled in college in 1985. This percentage, for the total age group, has shown relatively little change over the last 2 decades.

Among blacks, 26.1 percent of high-school graduates (between 18 and 24 years of age) were enrolled in college in 1985. This figure represents a decrease since 1976, when 33.5 percent were enrolled in college.

Among Hispanics, 26.9 percent of high-school graduates (between 18 and 24 years of age) were enrolled in college in 1985. This figure represents a decrease since 1976, when 35.8 percent were enrolled in college.

Source: *Current Population Reports,* P-20, no. 409, pp. 8–9.

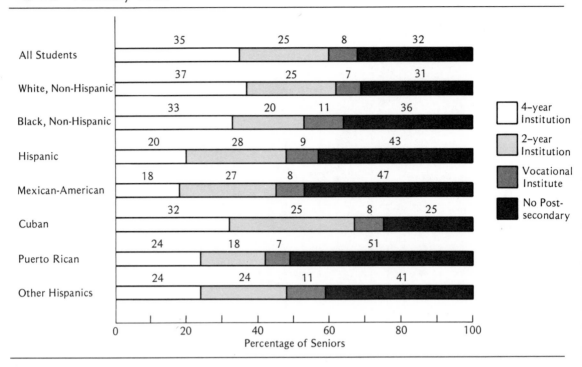

Among 1980 high-school seniors, 63 percent had enrolled for postsecondary study by February 1982.

Among these seniors, 25 percent entered a two-year college and 8 percent entered a vocational/technical institution. Another 35 percent entered a four-year college.[1]

The time that elapsed between high school and entry into postsecondary education differed according to type of institution attended. Among those that entered two-year colleges, 72 percent enrolled immediately after high school. This figure compares with 89 percent at four-year colleges and 62.5 percent at vocational/technical institutions.

Among these seniors, 25 percent of whites, 20 percent of blacks, and 28 percent of Hispanics entered two-year institutions.

Note: 1. Because some students entered more than one type of institution during this period, percentages on enrollment at different types of institutions sum to more than 63 percent, the overall percentage of students who enrolled for postsecondary study.

Sources: U.S. Department of Education, Center for Education Statistics, *Two Years after High School: A Capsule Description of 1980 Seniors* (High School and Beyond), 1984; *The Condition of Education, 1985,* pp. 228–229.

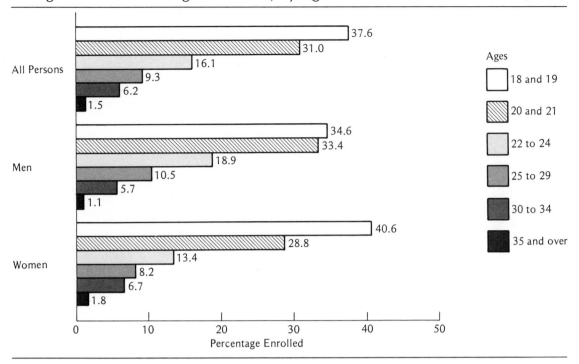

In 1983, 37.6 percent of 18–19-year-olds and 31.0 percent of 20–21-year-olds were enrolled in college.

In contrast, 9.3 percent of 25–29-year-olds and 6.2 percent of 30–34-year-olds were enrolled in college. Among persons 35 and over, 1.5 percent were enrolled in college.

Among 18–19-year-olds, 34.6 percent of men and 40.6 percent of women were enrolled in college. However, for persons between 20 and 29 years old, women were less likely than men to be enrolled in college.

Source: *Current Population Reports*, P-20, no. 413, pp. 56 and 70–71; Appendix Table A-23.

Full- and Part-Time Enrollment among U.S. Adults, by Age: 1983

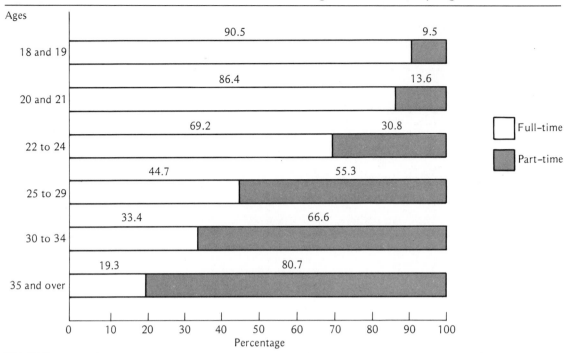

Among American adults enrolled in college in 1983, the majority of those over the age of 25 were enrolled part-time.

For persons over the age of 25, there were sizable differences in part-time status for different age groupings:

- Among adults 35 and over who were enrolled in college, four out of five were enrolled part-time.
- In contrast, among adults 25–29 years of age, just over half (55.3 percent) were enrolled part-time. Conversely, just under half (44.7 percent) of persons in this age group who were enrolled in college were attending on a full-time basis.

Among persons between the ages of 22–24 who were enrolled in college, 7 in 10 were attending on a full-time basis.

Source: *Current Population Reports,* P-20, no. 413, pp. 23 and 56; Appendix Table A-24.

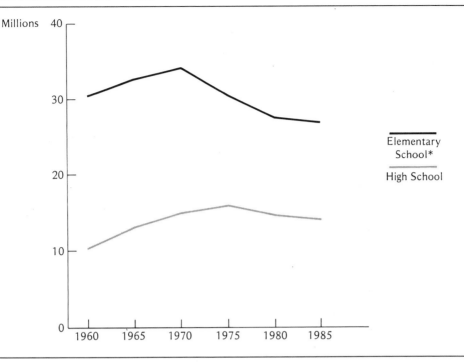

Elementary school enrollment[1] in 1985 (public and private) totaled 26,866,000. This figure is down 21 percent from a peak enrollment in 1970 of 33,950,000.

Elementary school enrollment will rise in the latter half of the 1980s because of increased births after 1975.

High-school enrollment in 1985 totaled 13,979,000, 11 percent fewer than the 15.7 million enrolled during the peak years of 1975–1979. High-school enrollment may rise after 1990 because of increased births after 1975, depending on variations in the dropout rate.

Private school enrollment accounts for 11.4 percent of elementary school enrollment (3.1 million students) and 8.7 percent of high-school enrollment (1.2 million students).

Note: 1. Does not include kindergarten enrollment.
Source: *Current Population Reports,* P-20, no. 409, p. 4; Appendix Table A-25.

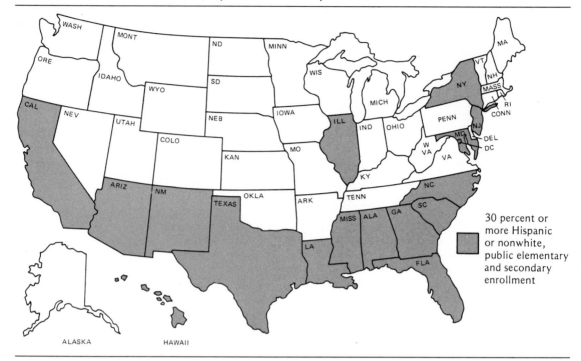

30 percent or more Hispanic or nonwhite, public elementary and secondary enrollment

Minorities comprise an increasing proportion of elementary and high-school enrollment.

In 1985, black and Hispanic youth comprised 16 percent and 10.4 percent, respectively, of elementary school enrollment.

Of high-school enrollment in 1985, black and Hispanic youth comprised 15.2 percent and 8.3 percent of enrollment, respectively.

Hispanic and nonwhite enrollment varies from state to state. The states with the largest percentages of Hispanic and nonwhite enrollment (public elementary and secondary schools) include the following:

Dist. Columbia	96.2	Maryland	41.8
Hawaii	76.9	South Carolina	41.4
New Mexico	55.1	Arizona	37.7
Mississippi	50.7	Georgia	37.0
California	48.0	Alabama	36.1
Louisiana	44.5	New York	35.6
Texas	43.4	Illinois	35.3
		New Jersey	30.1

Sources: *Current Population Reports*, P-20, no. 409, p. 4; *Digest of Education Statistics, 1987*, table 35, p, 46; Appendix Tables A-25 and A-26.

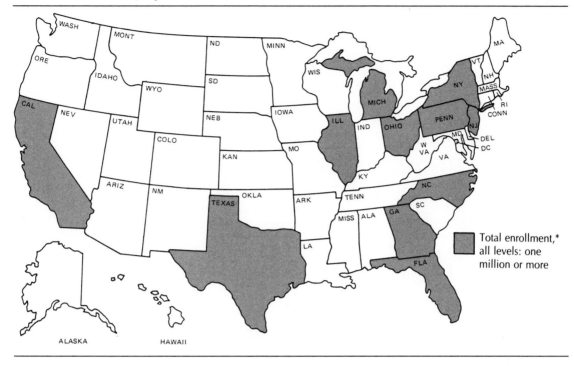

Total enrollment,* all levels: one million or more

The number of students enrolled in public elementary and secondary education* ranges widely, from a high of 4.3 million in California to lows of 90,157 in Vermont and 87,092 in the District of Columbia. Eleven states had public elementary and secondary enrollments of 1 million or more.

Seven states had public high-school enrollments (grades 9–12) in 1985 of more than 500,000 students:

California	1,328,849	Ohio	587,637
New York	917,948	Michigan	585,859
Texas	871,026	Illinois	579,982
Pennsylvania	590,663		

*Figures include nursery and kindergarten enrollment.

Source: *Digest of Education Statistics, 1987*, table 31, pp. 40–41; Appendix Table A-27.

50 High-School Graduates: 1977 to 1995

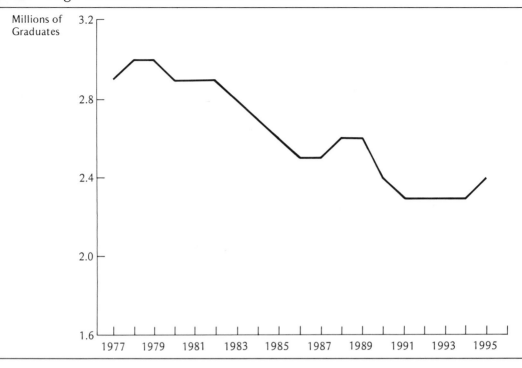

Millions of Graduates

The number of high-school graduates in the Untied States reached an all-time high in the late 1970s.

In the early 1980s, there have been small annual decreases in the number of high-school graduates, with a low of 2.51 million graduates (public and private) in 1985–86. Small yearly increases in the number of high-school graduates are expected in 1987 and 1988.

Sizable decreases in the number of high-school graduates are expected in 1990 and again in 1991. Between 1991 and 1994, about 2.3 million graduates yearly are expected.

There are some variations in this pattern for individual states and regions and for racial and ethnic groupings.

Note: Data shown in the figure include graduates of public and private high schools, but exclude high-school equivalency certificates. Data from the U.S. Department of Education (see Appendix Table A-28) are based only on graduates of public high schools.

Sources: Western Interstate Commission for Higher Education, *High School Graduates: Projections for the Fifty States 1982–2000*, 1984, and Update, June 25, 1987; *Digest of Education Statistics, 1987*, table 71, p. 85; Appendix Table A-28.

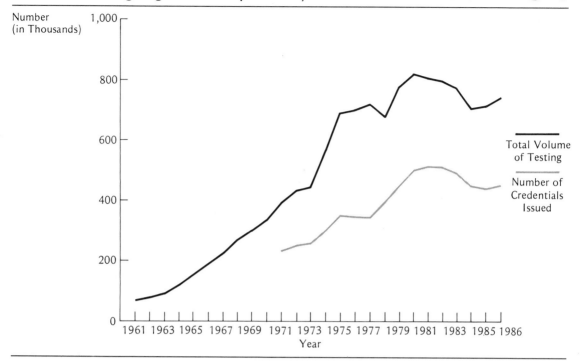

Number (in Thousands)

Total Volume of Testing

Number of Credentials Issued

Year

In 1986, a total of 451,294 high-school equivalency credentials were issued by the General Educational Development (GED) Testing Service. This represents about one out of every seven high-school diplomas issued in the United States.

The number of persons taking the GED test in 1986 totaled 739,683. More than half of test-takers planned to undertake further study. About 73 percent earned scores sufficient to qualify for the equivalency credential.

Of persons taking the GED test in 1986, 43 percent were between 20 and 29 years old, 18 percent were between 30 and 39 years of age, and about 11 percent were age 40 and over.

During 1986, 31,195 people took a Spanish-language edition of the GED test.

The six states testing the largest number of examinees were: New York (88,040), Texas (59,045), California (48,148), Florida (41,100), Illinois (29,971), and Michigan (27,604).

Since 1971, over 6 million adults have obtained high-school equivalency credentials through the GED program.

Source: General Educational Development Testing Service of the American Council on Education, *The 1986 GED Statistical Report,* pp. 20, 22.

High-School Completion Rates, Persons Age 18–24, by Race/Ethnicity: 1975–1985

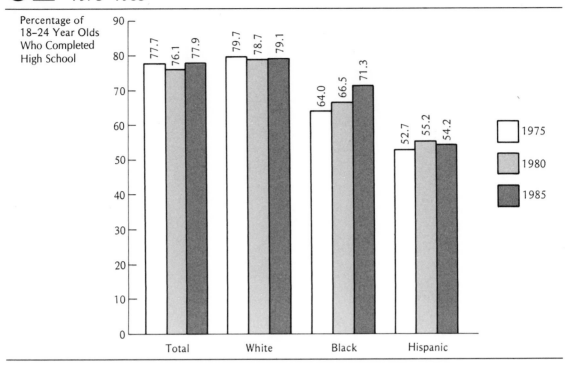

Percentage of 18–24 Year Olds Who Completed High School

	1975	1980	1985
Total	77.7	76.1	77.9
White	79.7	78.7	79.1
Black	64.0	66.5	71.3
Hispanic	52.7	55.2	54.2

Among young people between the ages of 18–24 in 1985, nearly 8 out of 10 were high-school graduates. This overall figure has changed very little during the last decade.

High-school completion rates for blacks between the ages of 18–24 have improved markedly since 1975. Seven out of ten blacks (71.3 percent) ages 18–24 completed high school in 1985, compared to 64 percent in 1975.

In 1985, the high-school completion rate for Hispanics (ages 18–24) was only 54.2 percent. This compares to 52.7 percent in 1975.

These rates, based on 18–24-year-olds, allow for the fact that a sizable number of young people do not complete high school at ages 18 or 19 but do obtain a high school diploma or its equivalent during the next few years. Thus, high-school completion rates among 18–19-year-olds in 1985 were as follows: all 18–19-year-olds, 62.0 percent; whites, 64.3 percent; blacks, 50.9 percent; and Hispanics, 40.4 percent.

Sources: *Current Population Reports*, P-20, no. 295, pp. 9–14; U.S. Census Bureau, *1980 Census of Population, Detailed Population Characteristics*, U.S. Summary, Section A, table 262; *Digest of Education Statistics, 1987*, table 9, pp. 14–15.

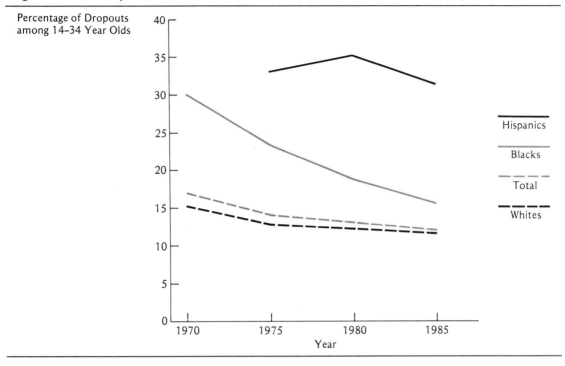

Percentage of Dropouts among 14–34 Year Olds

Hispanics

Blacks

Total

Whites

Year

Among persons 14–34 years of age in 1985, 12.0 percent were considered high-school dropouts—that is, they were not enrolled in school and did not have a high-school diploma or its equivalent.

Since 1970, dropout rates have declined steadily, both for the population as a whole and for black Americans. In 1985, 15.5 percent of blacks were high-school dropouts, compared to 30.0 in 1970.

Dropout rates for Hispanics were considerably higher, 31.4 percent in 1985.

Because of the aging of the "Baby Boom" generation, the actual number of high-school dropouts in this segment of the population has been decreasing since 1981.

Sources: *Digest of Education Statistics, 1987,* table 72, p. 86; *Current Population Reports,* P-20, no. 409, p. 4; Appendix Table A-29.

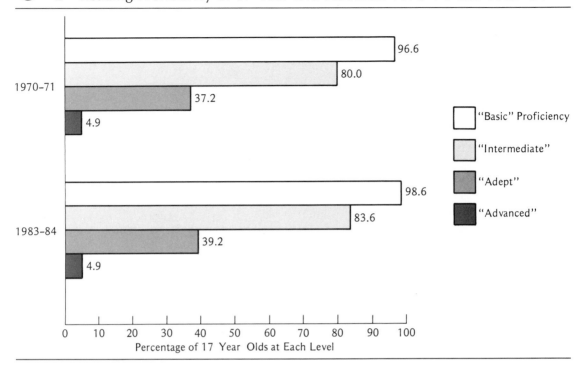

Percentage of 17 Year Olds at Each Level

In 1983–84, more than 8 in 10 American 17-year-old students had reading skills rated at an "intermediate level" by the National Assessment of Educational Progress (NAEP). This rating requires an ability to search for specific information, interrelate ideas, and make generalizations about literature, science, and social studies materials.

Only 39.2 percent of 17-year-olds tested, according to NAEP, read at an "adept" level, that is, are able to find, understand, summarize, and explain relatively complicated literary and informational material. Another 4.9 percent were at the "advanced" level.

At each level, 1983–84 results showed small gains over scores of 17-year-olds in 1970–71, when the test was first administered.

Differences in reading proficiency were related to socioeconomic background of students. Students who lived in disadvantaged metropolitan areas or whose parents did not graduate from high school had lower scores than other students.

Sources: *Digest of Education Statistics, 1987,* table 74, p. 88; U.S. Department of Education, National Assessment of Educational Progress, *The Reading Report Card.*

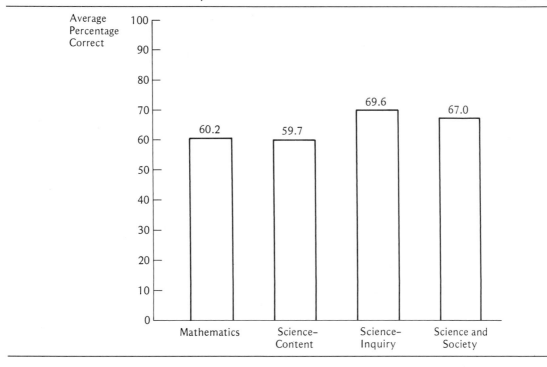

Nationally, American 17-year-olds participating in the National Assessment of Educational Progress (NAEP) answered about 60 percent correct on a mathematics test conducted by NAEP in 1981–82. This average level of mathematics proficiency was also reported in 1977–78.

Only small differences in mathematics proficiency appeared between male and female 17-year-olds (average scores of 61.6 and 58.9, respectively), but racial/ethnic differences were sizable: the average for black youth was 45.0, the average for Hispanic youth was 49.4, and the average for white youth was 63.1.

NAEP scores on science proficiency showed an overall average of 59.7 for science content, with small differences between males and females (62.7 versus 56.9 percent, respectively). Differences by racial/ethnic background also appeared.

The average scores on areas of science inquiry and on science and society were higher, at 69.6 and 67.0, respectively. Differences by gender were quite small on these scores (1–3 percentage points), although sizable racial/ethnic differences appeared.

Sources: *Digest of Education Statistics, 1987,* tables 75 and 76, pp. 89–90; U.S. Department of Education, National Assessment of Educational Progress, unpublished tabulations.

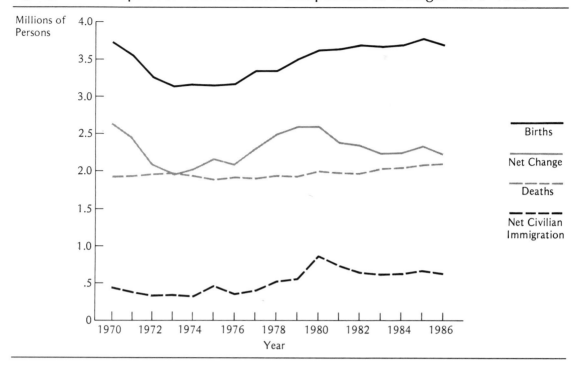

The total U.S. population (including armed forces overseas) was estimated to be 243,571,000 as of June 1, 1987. The resident population totaled 243,050,000 as of this date.

The U.S. population increased by 2.2 million persons (0.9 percent) during calendar year 1986. This resulted from a natural increase (i.e., births minus deaths) of 1.6 million persons and net civilian immigration of 625,000.

About 28 percent of the population change in 1986 resulted from immigration. Immigrants from Asia were 46.4 percent of all immigrants in 1986.

There were 3.7 million births in 1986. The number of births has been increasing since 1976, following a 15-year period of decline between 1960 and 1975.

There were 2.1 million deaths in 1986, continuing the small increases that have occurred each year since 1982. These increases are due to the aging of the U.S. population.

The median age of the U.S. population was 31.5 years in 1985 and is projected to reach 36.3 years by 2000. In 1970, the median age was 27.9 years.

Source: *Current Population Reports,* P-25, nos. 1006 and 1008.

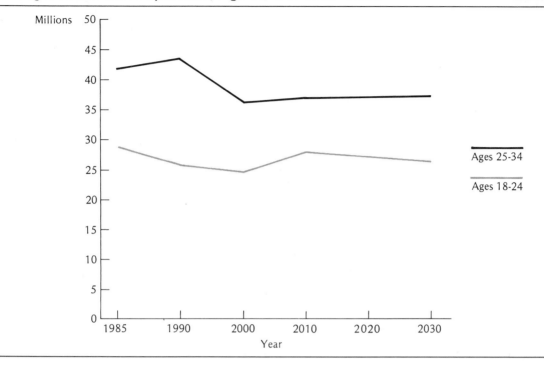

Two age groups that generate large numbers of college students—persons between 18 and 24 years of age and persons between 25 and 34 years of age—are expected to decrease in size over the next 4 decades.

These age groups comprised 29.5 percent of the population in 1985, but will comprise 20.8 percent of the population in 2030 (based on "middle-series" projections of the U.S. Census Bureau).

The 18–24-year-old age group will decrease 9 percent by 2030. This age group will comprise only 8.6 percent of the population in 2030, down from 12 percent in 1985.

The 25–34-year-old age group will decrease 11 percent by 2030. In 2030, this age group will represent 12.2 percent of the population, down from 17.5 percent in 1985.

Source: *Current Population Reports,* P-25, no. 952, pp. 7–8; Appendix Table A-30.

58 Changes in the U.S. Population Age 45 and Over: 1985–2030

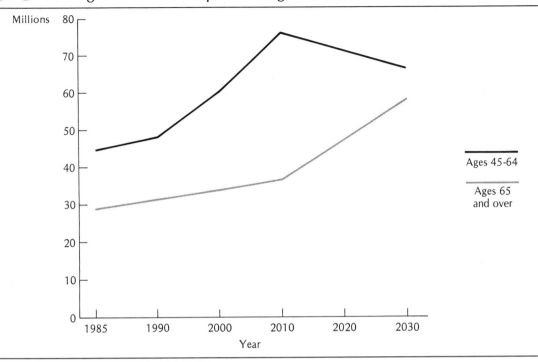

Older Americans will comprise an increasing share of the population during the next 4 decades. Persons 45 and over will make up 44.3 percent of the population in 2030, up from 30.7 percent in 1985 (based on "middle-series" projections of the U.S. Census Bureau).

Persons age 65 and over will double in number, from 28.6 million to 58.1 million by 2030. Most of this increase will occur after 2010, as members of the Baby Boom generation reach age 65. This age group will represent 21.2 percent of the population in 2030, up from 12 percent in 1985.

Persons 45–64 years of age will increase by 49 percent, from 44.6 million in 1985 to 66.6 million in 2030. According to "middle-series" projections of the Census Bureau, 23.2 percent of the population will be in this age group in 2030, up from 18.7 percent in 1985.

A total of 2.7 million persons were 85 years and over in 1985. By 2030, this number is expected to increase to 8.6 million.

Source: *Current Population Reports,* P-25, no. 952, pp. 7–8; Appendix Table A-30.

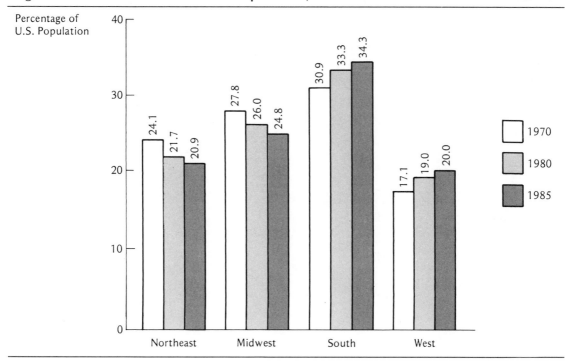

Percentage of U.S. Population

40

30

20

10

0

Northeast   Midwest   South   West

Northeast: 24.1, 21.7, 20.9
Midwest: 27.8, 26.0, 24.8
South: 30.9, 33.3, 34.3
West: 17.1, 19.0, 20.0

☐ 1970
◻ 1980
◼ 1985

The population of the United States continues to shift toward the South and the West. In 1985, it was estimated that 34.3 percent of the U.S. population lived in the South and 20 percent of the population lived in the West.

Nine states—all in the South or West—had population growth of 10 percent or more between 1980 and 1985, as follows:

Alaska	29.7	Utah	12.6
Arizona	17.2	Colorado	11.8
Nevada	16.9	California	11.4
Florida	16.6	New Mexico	11.3
Texas	15.0		

Population grew by 10.8 percent in the West and by 8.6 percent in the South between 1980 and 1985.

Sources: *Current Population Reports,* P-25, no. 957, October 1984, p. 13; *Statistical Abstract, 1987,* tables 23 and 27, pp. 19 and 24.

Projected Changes in State Populations: 1990–2000

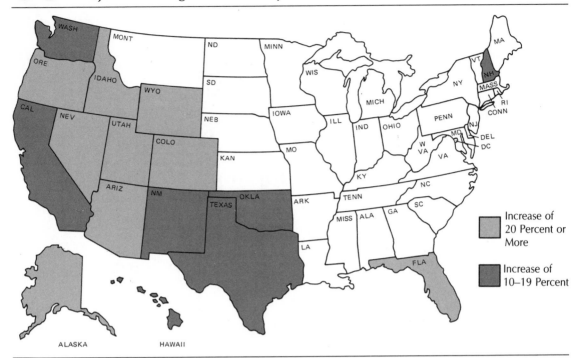

Between 1990 and 2000, the U.S. population is expected to increase by 7.3 percent. Sixteen states are projected to grow by 10 percent or more, and eleven states will lose population between 1990 and 2000.

Nevada will be the most rapidly growing state in the next decade (a projected gain of 50.4 percent). Increases of more than 35 percent are also expected for Wyoming, Arizona, and Utah.

Eleven states and the District of Columbia are projected to lose population between 1990 and 2000. Large decreases are expected for the District of Columbia (−25 percent) and New York (−8.9 percent). Ten other states will lose 4 percent or fewer over the next decade.

Florida, California, and Texas each will add more than 3 million persons to their populations between 1990 and 2000, more than any other states.

California is expected to continue to be the largest state, with 30.6 million people, or 11.5 percent of the U.S. population in 2000. If present trends continue, Texas will be the second largest state in 2000 (7.8 percent of the U.S. population), and Florida will become the third largest state (6.5 percent of the U.S. population), with New York moving to fourth place (with an expected 5.6 percent of the population in 2000).

Source: *Current Population Reports,* P-25, no. 937, p. 11; Appendix Table A-31.

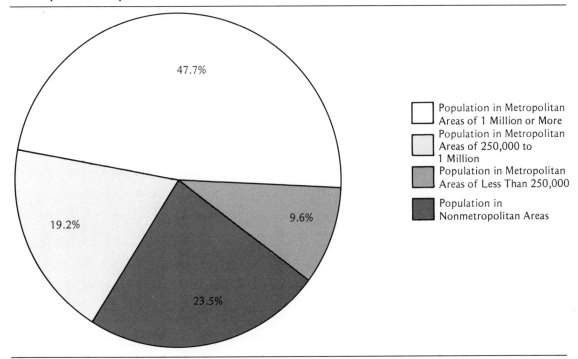

47.7%

19.2%

9.6%

23.5%

☐ Population in Metropolitan Areas of 1 Million or More

▨ Population in Metropolitan Areas of 250,000 to 1 Million

▨ Population in Metropolitan Areas of Less Than 250,000

▨ Population in Nonmetropolitan Areas

In 1985, 76.5 percent of the U.S. population lived in metropolitan areas.

By 1985, almost half of the population (47.7 percent) lived in the 35 metropolitan areas with populations of 1 million or more, reflecting an increasing urban concentration of the population. In 1950, only 29 percent of the population lived in the 14 metropolitan areas with 1 million or more persons.

Since 1980, nearly 20 percent of metropolitan areas (primarily those of less than 500,000 persons) lost population. Sixteen metropolitan areas grew by 3 percent or more annually since 1980.

The nonmetropolitan population totals 56.2 million persons, or 23.5 percent of the population. Most live in the South (25 million persons) or Midwest (17.4 million persons).

There were about 5.4 million persons living on farms in the United States in 1985, comprising 2.2 percent of the population. In 1920, 30 percent of the population lived on farms. Only about half of employed farm residents worked solely or primarily in agriculture in 1985.

Sources: *Statistical Abstract, 1987,* tables 31, 33, and 34, pp. 26–30; *Current Population Reports,* P-23, no. 150, pp. 14–17; Appendix Table A-32.

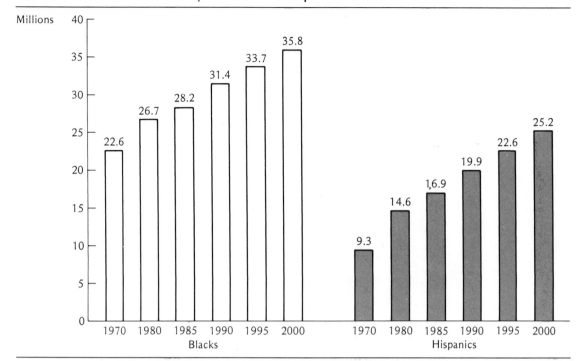

In March 1985, the U.S. population included an estimated 28,151,000 blacks (12 percent of the population) and 16,940,000 Hispanics (7.2 percent of the population).

Both of these groups are growing faster than the population as a whole. By the year 2000, blacks are projected to total 35,753,000, or 13.3 percent of the U.S. population (based on "middle-series" projections of the U.S. Census Bureau). Hispanics are projected to total 25,223,000, or 9.4 percent of the U.S. population by the year 2000.

Persons of "other races" (principally Asians, Pacific Islanders, and American Indians) totaled 7.1 million in 1985. This population group grew by 37.5 percent between 1980 and July 1985, primarily due to immigration.

Source: *Statistical Abstract, 1987,* tables 16, 19, 20, and 39, pp. 16–18 and 35; Appendix Tables A-33 and A-34.

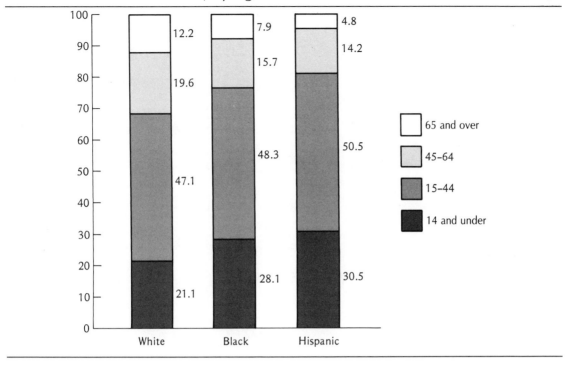

Blacks and Hispanics were younger than the white population of the United States in the mid-1980s.

Among blacks, children 14 years old and younger accounted for 28.1 percent of the population group in 1985. Among Hispanics, 30.5 percent were 14 years or younger.

Conversely, these minority populations have smaller proportions of persons age 65 and over. Only 4.8 percent of Hispanics were 65 and over in 1985. Among blacks, 7.9 percent were age 65 and over in 1985.

A relatively "young" age profile is also found among persons of "other races" (principally Asians, Pacific Islanders, and American Indians).

This age distribution of minority populations is expected to continue over the next 2 decades.

Source: *Statistical Abstract, 1987,* table 39, p. 35; Appendix Tables A-33 and A-34.

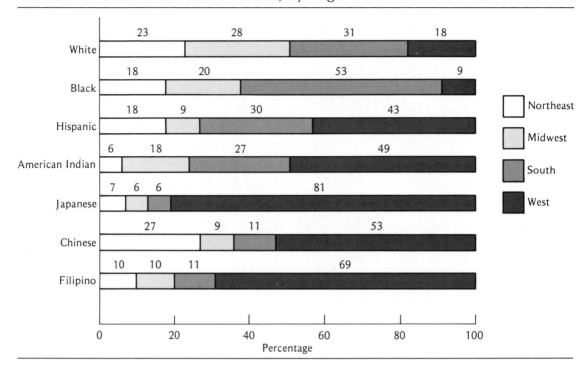

Most racial and ethnic groups in the United States had quite distinctive patterns of regional distribution in 1980.

More than half of blacks lived in the South in 1980, with another 20 percent in the Midwest.

Hispanics were located primarily in the West (43 percent) and the South (30 percent), with 18 percent in the Northeast states.

Persons of Japanese, Chinese, and Filipino origin were located predominantly in the Western states. Another 27 percent of Chinese persons were located in the Northeast states.

About half of American Indians (49 percent) lived in the Western states in 1980, with another 27 percent living in the South and 18 percent in the Midwest.

Source: U.S. Census Bureau, *1980 Census of Population, Vol. 1: Characteristics of the Population,* PC 80–1, September 1981; Appendix Table A-35.

65

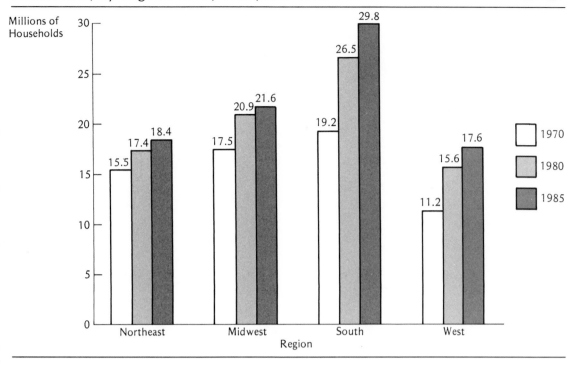

Millions of Households

The number of households in the United States increased by 2.4 percent annually between 1970 and 1980, and by 1.6 percent annually between 1980 and 1985.

The average number of households in the West increased 3.3 percent between 1970 and 1980, and 2.4 percent between 1980 and 1985. This region had the highest average annual increase during both periods.

With the exception of Alaska, all states experienced a slower annual growth rate for the number of households between 1980 and 1985 than during the earlier 10-year period.

Source: *Statistical Abstract 1987*, table 63, p. 46; Appendix Table A-36.

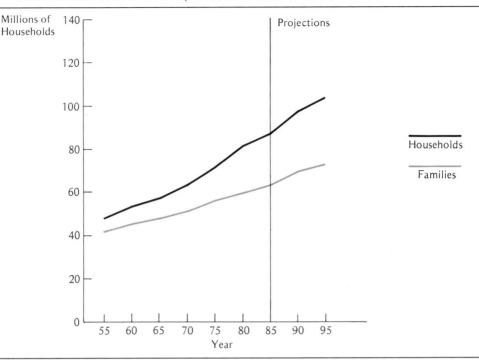

The number of households increased by 1.4 million between March 1984 and March 1985, a slightly higher yearly increase than occurred between 1980 and 1985.

The 1985 rate of increase in total households was down 23 percent from the 1.6 million annual increase that took place during the 1970s.

By 1995, the number of households is projected to increase to 104 million from the 1985 level of 87 million.

The average number of persons per household in 1985 was 2.69. This figure is projected to drop still further to 2.39 by 1995.

In 1985, 63 million households (72 percent) contained families. This figure was down slightly from 74 percent in 1980 and 78 percent in 1975.

In 1985, the average number of children per family under the age of 18 was slightly less than one.

Sources: ACE, *1986–87 Fact Book on Higher Education,* p. 10; *Current Population Reports* P-20, no. 411, table 1 and 21, pp. 13–14, and 21; Appendix Table A-37.

Family Income, by Race/Ethnicity: 1985

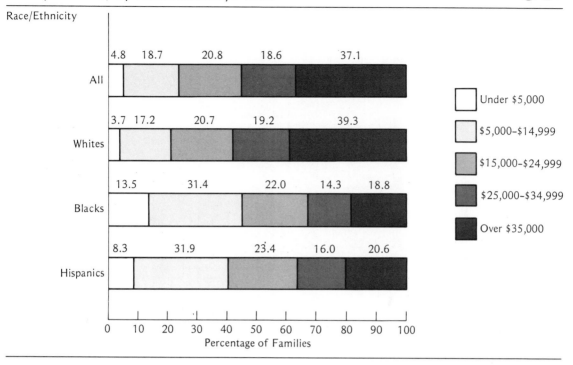

Race/Ethnicity

All
4.8 | 18.7 | 20.8 | 18.6 | 37.1

Whites
3.7 | 17.2 | 20.7 | 19.2 | 39.3

Blacks
13.5 | 31.4 | 22.0 | 14.3 | 18.8

Hispanics
8.3 | 31.9 | 23.4 | 16.0 | 20.6

Legend:
- ☐ Under $5,000
- ☐ $5,000–$14,999
- ▨ $15,000–$24,999
- ▨ $25,000–$34,999
- ■ Over $35,000

0 10 20 30 40 50 60 70 80 90 100
Percentage of Families

In 1985, approximately 24 percent of all families had incomes under $15,000. This figure was considerably higher for blacks and Hispanics (45 percent and 40 percent, respectively).

Fifty-nine percent of all white families had a family income of over $25,000, compared to 37 percent of all Hispanic families and 33 percent of all black families.

Between 1975 and 1985, the percentage of black families with incomes under $5,000 (in constant 1985 dollars) increased from 8.5 percent to 13.5 percent. Hispanic families with similar income levels increased from 6.5 percent in 1975 to 8.3 percent in 1985.

Source: *Statistical Abstract, 1987,* table 731, p. 436; Appendix Table A-38.

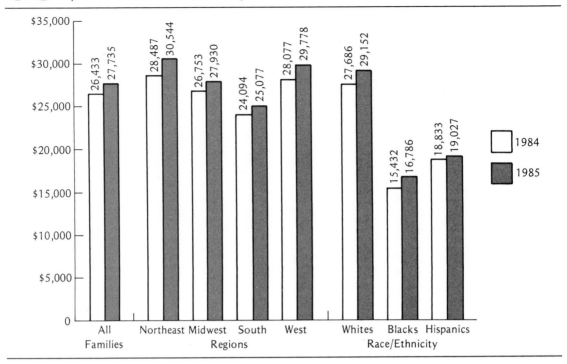

The median income for all families in 1985 was $27,735. In 1985 dollars, the median income was up 1.3 percent in 1985 over 1984.

The median family income in 1985 varied considerably by region:

Northeast	$30,544
Midwest	$27,930
South	$25,077
West	$29,778

There were sizable differences in 1985 family income according to race/ethnicity:

White families	$29,152
Black families	$16,786
Hispanic families	$19,027

Hispanic families experienced a 2.5 percent drop in income between 1984 and 1985, while the median income for white and black families rose 1.7 percent and 5.0 percent, respectively.

After adjusting for inflation between 1984 and 1985, the median family income increased 3.5 percent in the northeastern section of the country and 2.4 percent in the western states, and remained relatively constant in southern and midwestern states.

Source: *Current Population Reports*, P-60, 154, table 1, pp. 6–8.

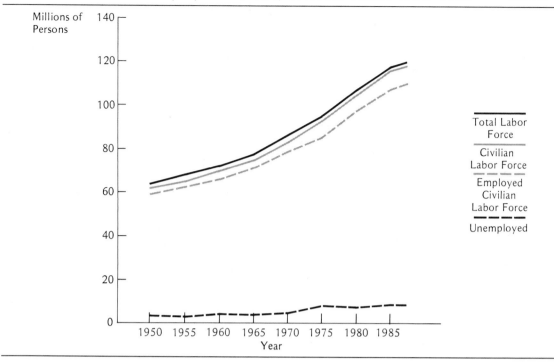

The total U.S. labor force in 1986 was 120 million. This was up from 97 million in 1976 and 110 million in 1981. The total labor force was nearly 66 percent of the noninstitutional population in 1986.

In 1986, nearly 118 million people were in the civilian labor force, compared to 115 million in 1985.

The annual unemployment rate dropped from 7.1 percent in 1985 to 6.9 percent in 1986. A total of 8.3 million people were out of work in 1985, compared to 8.2 million in 1986.

Sources: ACE, *1986–87 Fact Book on Higher Education*, table 34; BLS *Monthly Labor Review,* Vol. 110, no. 7, pp. 62–63; Appendix Table A-39.

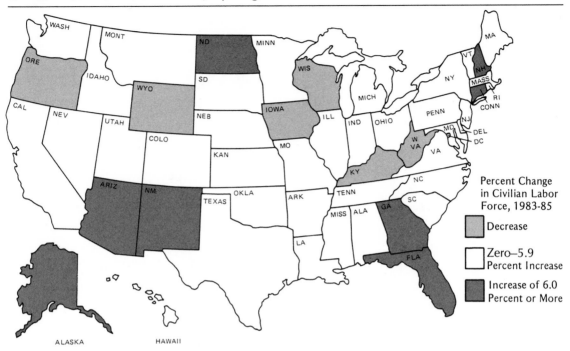

Percent Change in Civilian Labor Force, 1983-85

Decrease

Zero–5.9 Percent Increase

Increase of 6.0 Percent or More

Between 1983 and 1985, the southwestern states experienced the highest regional growth rate in the civilian labor force, 8.7 percent.

Between 1983 and 1985, the Great Lake region had the slowest civilian labor force growth rate, 1.2 percent.

The civilian labor force in the following six states and the District of Columbia declined between 1983 and 1985:

Kentucky	Iowa
West Virginia	Wyoming
Wisconsin	Oregon

The size of the civilian labor force in all other states increased.

Sources: ACE, *1986–87 Fact Book on Higher Education*, pp. 32–33; *Statistical Abstract, 1987* table 641, p. 377; Appendix Table A-40.

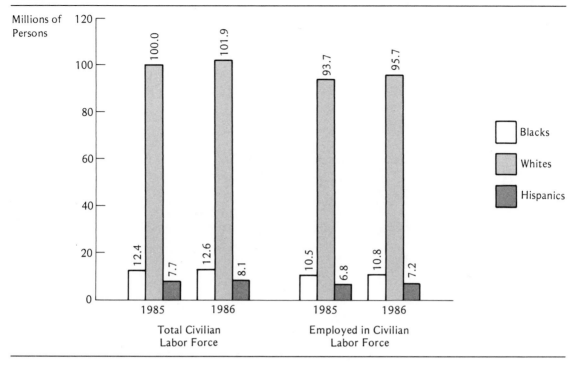

Millions of Persons

Total Civilian Labor Force — 1985, 1986

Blacks: 12.4, 12.6
Whites: 100.0, 101.9
Hispanics: 7.7, 8.1

Employed in Civilian Labor Force — 1985, 1986

Blacks: 10.5, 10.8
Whites: 93.7, 95.7
Hispanics: 6.8, 7.2

In 1986, there were 102 million whites, 13 million blacks, and 8 million Hispanics in the civilian labor force.

The participation rate in the civilian labor force was 65 percent for whites and Hispanics and 64 percent for blacks.

The unemployment rate varied significantly by race/ethnicity:

Whites	6	percent
Blacks	15	percent
Hispanics	11	percent

Between 1985 and 1986, the unemployment rate for whites and blacks declined slightly, while it increased slightly for Hispanics.

Note: Detail for race and Hispanic-origin groups will not sum to totals because data for the "other races" are not present, and Hispanics are included in both white and black population groups.
Source: BLS, *Monthly Labor Review*, May 1987, table 5, pp. 62–63.

72 Civilian Employment by Broad Occupation Group: 1986 and Moderate Projection Alternatives for 2000

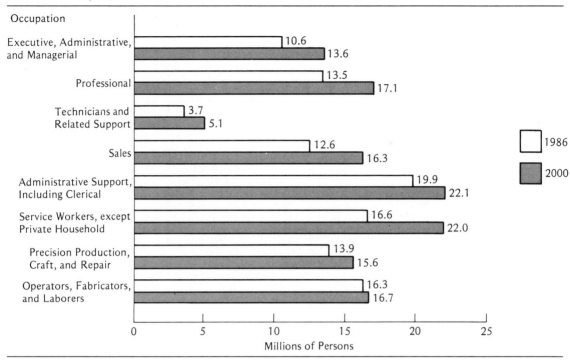

Based on moderate series projections of the Bureau of Labor Statistics, the number of persons employed is expected to increase 19 percent by 2000.

Between 1986 and 2000, employment in occupations requiring more education are projected to increase faster than those that require less education. Professional occupations will increase 27 percent; the number of executive, administrative, and managerial employees will increase 29 percent.

The number of college and university faculty is projected to drop 4 percent between 1986 and 2000.

Of the occupations requiring less education, service workers are projected to increase 33 percent, compared to 12 percent for precision production, craft, and repair workers, and only 2.6 percent for operators, fabricators, and laborers.

By 2000, the following growth is projected in these selected occupations:

Computer system analysts	76 percent
Computer programmers	70 percent
Teachers: kindergarten and elementary	20 percent
Electrical and electronics engineering	49 percent
Registered nurses	44 percent

Source: BLS, *Previews of the Economy of the Year 2000*, table 5; Appendix Table A-41.

Unemployment Rate of the Civilian Labor Force, by State: 1986

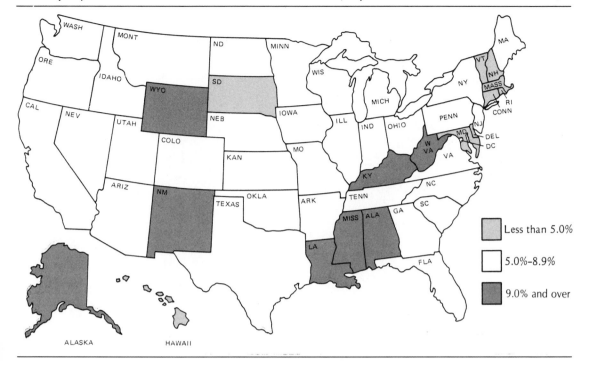

Less than 5.0%

5.0%–8.9%

9.0% and over

In 1986, the national rate of civilian labor-force unemployment was 7.0 percent. Unemployment rates in different regions of the country were as follows:

Northeast	5.6 percent
Midwest	7.3 percent
South	7.6 percent
West	7.1 percent

The unemployment rate was highest for women in the South and the Midwest, 8.0 percent. Unemployment for men was highest in the Midwest, 7.3 percent.

States with the highest unemployment rates in the civilian labor force in 1986 were the following:

Louisiana	13.1 percent	Alabama	9.8 percent
West Virginia	11.8 percent	Kentucky	9.3 percent
Mississippi	11.7 percent	New Mexico	9.3 percent
Alaska	10.8 percent	Wyoming	9.0 percent

As of 1986 the following states had unemployment rates below 5 percent:

New Hampshire	2.8 percent	Maryland	4.5 percent
Connecticut	3.8 percent	South Dakota	4.7 percent
Massachusetts	3.8 percent	Vermont	4.7 percent
Rhode Island	4.0 percent	Hawaii	4.8 percent
Delaware	4.3 percent		

Source: *Geographic Profile of Employment and Unemployment, 1986,* no. 2279, table 12, pp. 39–48.

Appendix

Total First-Time-Freshmen Enrollment in Institutions of Higher Education, by Sex of Student, Attendance Status, and Type and Control of Institution: Fall 1955–Fall 1985 (in Thousands)

A-1

		Men			Women			Type of Institution, by Control			
								Four-Year		Two-Year	
Year	Total Enrollment	Total	Full-Time	Part-Time	Total	Full-Time	Part-Time	Public	Private	Public	Private
1	2	3	4	5	6	7	8	9	10	11	12
1955[1]	670	416	—	—	254	—	—	[2]283	[2]247	[2]117	[2]23
1956[1]	718	443	—	—	275	—	—	[2]293	[2]262	[2]137	[2]25
1957[1]	724	442	—	—	282	—	—	[2]294	[2]263	[2]141	[2]27
1958[1]	775	465	—	—	310	—	—	[2]328	[2]272	[2]146	[2]29
1959[1]	822	488	—	—	334	—	—	[2]348	[2]292	[2]153	[2]28
1960[1]	923	540	—	—	384	—	—	[2]396	[2]313	[2]182	[2]32
1961[1]	1,018	592	—	—	426	—	—	[2]438	[2]336	[2]210	[2]34
1962[1]	1,031	598	—	—	432	—	—	[2]445	[2]325	[2]225	[2]36
1963[1]	1,046	604	—	—	442	—	—	—	—	—	—
1964[1]	1,225	702	—	—	523	—	—	[2]539	[2]363	[2]275	[2]47
1965[1]	1,442	829	—	—	613	—	—	[2]642	[2]399	[2]348	[2]53
1966	1,554	890	—	—	665	—	—	[2]626	[2]383	[2]478	[2]67
1967	1,641	931	761	170	710	574	136	[2]645	[2]368	[2]561	[2]67
1968	1,893	1,082	847	235	810	624	187	[2]725	[2]378	[2]718	[2]72
1969	1,967	1,118	876	242	849	649	200	[2]737	[2]393	[2]776	[2]61
1970	2,063	1,152	896	256	911	691	221	[2]754	[2]397	[2]854	[2]58
1971	2,119	1,171	896	275	949	710	238	[2]738	[2]386	[2]937	[2]58
1972	2,153	1,158	858	299	995	716	279	680	381	1,037	55
1973	2,226	1,182	867	315	1,044	740	304	699	379	1,089	59
1974	2,366	1,244	896	348	1,122	777	345	746	386	1,176	58
1975	2,515	1,328	942	386	1,187	821	366	772	395	1,284	64
1976	2,347	1,170	855	316	1,177	808	369	717	414	1,153	63
1977	2,394	1,156	840	316	1,239	841	398	737	405	1,186	67
1978	2,390	1,142	817	324	1,248	834	414	737	407	1,174	73
1979	2,503	1,180	840	340	1,323	866	457	760	415	1,254	74
1980	2,588	1,219	862	357	1,369	887	481	765	418	1,314	91
1981	2,595	1,218	852	366	1,378	886	492	754	419	1,318	104
1982	2,505	1,199	837	362	1,306	851	455	731	404	1,254	116
1983	2,444	1,159	825	334	1,285	853	431	728	404	1,190	122
1984	2,357	1,112	786	326	1,245	827	418	714	403	1,130	110
1985	2,292	1,076	775	301	1,216	827	389	717	399	1,060	116

Note. Alaska and Hawaii are included in all years. Because of rounding, details may not add to totals.

1 Excludes first-time freshmen in occupational programs not creditable toward a bachelor's degree.

2 Data for two-year branches of four-year college systems are aggregated with the four-year institutions.

— Data not available.

Source: *Digest of Education Statistics, 1987,* no. 110, p. 130.

A-2

College Enrollment of Students* 14–34 Years Old, by Type of College, Attendance Status, Age, and Sex: October 1970–1985

Age, Sex, Full-Time Status, and Type of College	1970	1975	1976	1977	1978	1979	1980	1981[2]	1981[1]	1982	1983	1984	1985
ALL COLLEGE STUDENTS													
Total, 14–34 years	7,413	9,697	9,950	10,218	9,839	9,978	10,180	10,437	10,734	10,919	10,825	10,859	10,863
ALL UNDERGRADUATES													
Total, 14–34 years	6,274	8,108	8,270	8,408	8,158	8,287	8,488	8,819	9,053	9,110	9,012	9,058	9,114
14–19 years	2,854	3,237	3,216	3,184	3,173	3,156	3,182	3,250	3,276	3,183	3,200	3,120	3,169
20–21 years	1,803	2,255	2,358	2,376	2,247	2,308	2,393	2,451	2,511	2,657	2,464	2,565	2,586
22–24 years	866	1,072	1,224	1,206	1,233	1,297	1,316	1,387	1,458	1,526	1,475	1,547	1,475
25–34 years	750	1,546	1,472	1,640	1,506	1,526	1,599	1,731	1,808	1,745	1,873	1,828	1,884
Public	4,910	6,598	6,578	6,683	6,340	6,541	(NA)	6,833	7,035	7,174	7,014	7,242	7,211
Private	1,363	1,510	1,692	1,724	1,816	1,746	(NA)	1,985	2,018	1,935	1,998	1,816	1,903
Male, 14–34 years	3,627	4,393	4,301	4,372	4,188	4,106	4,111	4,303	4,443	4,450	4,488	4,506	4,385
Full time	3,045	3,394	3,291	3,304	3,221	3,163	3,192	3,303	3,397	3,451	3,417	3,519	3,402
Part time	582	999	1,010	1,068	967	943	920	1,000	1,046	999	1,071	987	984
Female, 14–34 years	2,646	3,715	3,969	4,027	3,969	4,183	4,377	4,517	4,610	4,660	4,525	4,551	4,728
Full time	2,164	2,902	3,090	3,002	2,948	3,051	3,123	3,285	3,343	3,355	3,314	3,302	3,452
Part time	482	813	879	1,025	1,021	1,132	1,254	1,231	1,266	1,305	1,211	1,249	1,276
Full Time													
Total, 14–34 years	5,208	6,296	6,381	6,304	6,169	6,225	6,315	6,588	6,740	6,807	6,729	6,823	6,854
14–19 years	2,685	2,987	2,963	2,855	2,872	2,892	2,897	2,960	2,983	2,880	2,895	2,846	2,900
20–21 years	1,628	1,958	2,033	2,075	1,919	1,994	2,107	2,106	2,157	2,286	2,124	2,221	2,237
22–24 years	591	696	821	775	821	814	810	937	986	979	993	1,067	1,017
25–34 years	301	655	563	598	559	525	500	585	613	662	718	689	701
Part Time													
Total, 14–34 years	1,066	1,812	1,889	2,104	1,988	2,062	2,173	2,231	2,312	2,304	2,282	2,237	2,259
14–19 years	169	250	253	329	302	264	282	291	293	302	305	274	269
20–21 years	175	297	325	301	328	314	286	343	353	372	340	344	349
22–24 years	275	376	403	431	412	483	505	450	471	547	482	480	457
25–34 years	449	891	909	1,042	947	1,001	1,098	1,146	1,195	1,083	1,153	1,139	1,184
TWO-YEAR COLLEGE STUDENTS													
Total, 14–34 years	1,692	2,561	2,435	2,510	2,453	2,407	2,666	2,801	2,892	3,011	2,931	2,756	2,772
14–19 years	895	1,024	907	933	966	933	1,080	1,125	1,144	1,088	1,050	994	959
20–21 years	281	431	444	455	427	403	450	549	566	604	595	525	558
22–24 years	234	354	367	380	391	407	417	392	414	494	405	442	403
25–34 years	283	752	718	741	670	664	721	735	768	826	882	795	851
Public	1,559	2,437	2,282	2,362	2,247	2,233	(NA)	2,559	2,646	2,750	2,663	2,496	2,516
Private	133	123	153	148	206	174	(NA)	241	245	260	268	260	256

	C1	C2	C3	C4	C5	C6	C7	C8	C9	C10	C11	C12	C13
Male, 14–34 years	1,179	1,333	1,370	1,359	1,333	1,280	1,195	1,106	1,214	1,253	1,272	1,412	1,001
Full time	678	812	786	832	801	773	739	661	679	681	734	850	726
Part time	501	521	584	527	532	506	456	445	535	572	538	562	275
Female, 14–34 years	1,593	1,422	1,560	1,652	1,559	1,521	1,472	1,301	1,239	1,256	1,163	1,148	691
Full time	860	766	852	905	842	825	759	680	664	691	696	717	452
Part time	733	656	709	747	717	696	713	621	575	565	467	431	239
Full Time													
Total, 14–34 years	1,538	1,579	1,638	1,737	1,643	1,599	1,498	1,341	1,343	1,372	1,430	1,567	1,177
14–19 years	779	812	855	883	927	910	884	749	778	718	764	865	786
20–21 years	341	330	374	381	357	346	287	251	243	283	261	274	197
22–24 years	174	190	159	214	170	162	160	156	157	162	177	155	114
25–34 years	244	247	250	260	188	181	167	185	167	208	228	274	80
Part Time													
Total, 14–34 years	1,234	1,177	1,293	1,274	1,249	1,202	1,168	1,066	1,110	1,138	1,005	994	515
14–19 years	180	182	195	206	217	214	195	184	190	216	143	159	109
20–21 years	217	195	221	223	209	203	163	152	184	172	183	157	84
22–24 years	229	252	245	280	243	230	256	251	234	218	190	199	120
25–34 years	607	548	631	566	579	554	554	479	503	533	490	478	203
GRADUATE STUDENTS													
Total, 14–34 years	1,749	1,802	1,814	1,810	1,681	1,618	1,692	1,691	1,681	1,810	1,680	1,590	1,140
14–21 years	31	32	32	32	34	34	30	44	51	57	42	57	54
22–24 years	540	580	568	535	530	511	554	497	565	593	622	607	488
25–34 years	1,179	1,190	1,214	1,244	1,120	1,074	1,104	1,149	1,063	1,161	1,017	923	599
Public	1,168	1,225	1,171	1,180	1,124	1,078	(NA)	1,157	1,087	1,241	1,161	1,105	789
Private	581	576	643	630	558	540	(NA)	534	594	568	519	484	351
Male, 14–34 years	959	1,007	1,017	960	929	890	914	888	935	995	994	949	774
Full time	550	612	623	568	514	491	500	469	477	548	542	542	432
Part time	409	395	394	392	415	399	414	419	458	447	452	407	342
Female, 14–34 years	790	794	797	850	753	728	777	804	745	813	686	640	366
Full time	313	387	359	362	314	305	332	317	334	338	254	267	123
Part time	477	407	438	488	439	423	445	487	411	475	432	373	243

* In thousands. Civilian noninstitutional population.

1 Controlled to 1980 census.

2 Controlled to 1970 census.

Source: *Current Population Reports*, P-20, no. 409, table 5, p. 7.

A-3 Total Enrollment in Institutions of Higher Education, by Type of Institution and Race/Ethnicity of Student: United States: Fall 1976–Fall 1984

Type of Institution and Race/Ethnicity of Student	Number, in Thousands				Percentage Distribution			
	1976	1980	1982	1984[1]	1976	1980	1982	1984[1]
1	2	3	4	5	6	7	8	9
All institutions	10,986	12,087	12,388	12,162	100.0	100.0	100.0	100.0
White, non-Hispanic	9,076	9,833	9,997	9,767	82.6	81.4	80.7	80.3
Total minority	1,691	1,949	2,059	2,063	15.4	16.1	16.6	17.0
Black, non-Hispanic	1,033	1,107	1,101	1,070	9.4	9.2	8.9	8.8
Hispanic	384	472	519	529	3.5	3.9	4.2	4.3
Asian or Pacific Islander	198	286	351	382	1.8	2.4	2.8	3.1
American Indian/Alaskan Native	76	84	88	83	0.7	0.7	0.7	0.7
Nonresident alien	219	305	331	332	2.0	2.5	2.7	2.7
Four-year institutions	7,107	7,565	7,648	7,651	64.7	62.6	61.7	62.9
White, non-Hispanic	5,999	6,275	6,306	6,263	54.6	51.9	50.9	51.5
Total minority	931	1,050	1,073	1,108	8.5	8.7	8.7	9.1
Black, non-Hispanic	604	634	612	613	5.5	5.2	4.9	5.0
Hispanic	174	217	229	241	1.6	1.8	1.8	2.0
Asian or Pacific Islander	119	162	193	217	1.1	1.3	1.6	1.8
American Indian/Alaskan Native	35	37	39	37	0.3	0.3	0.3	0.3
Nonresident alien	177	241	270	280	1.6	2.0	2.2	2.3
Two-year institutions	3,879	4,521	4,740	4,511	35.3	37.4	38.3	37.1
White, non-Hispanic	3,077	3,558	3,692	3,504	28.0	29.4	29.8	28.8
Total minority	760	899	987	955	6.9	7.4	8.0	7.8
Black, non-Hispanic	429	472	489	457	3.9	3.9	3.9	3.8
Hispanic	210	255	291	288	1.9	2.1	2.3	2.4
Asian or Pacific Islander	79	124	158	165	0.7	1.0	1.3	1.4
American Indian/Alaskan Native	41	47	49	45	0.4	0.4	0.4	0.4
Nonresident alien	42	64	61	52	0.4	0.5	0.5	0.4

Note: Because of underreporting and nonreporting of racial/ethnic data, totals in this table may be slightly smaller than totals appearing in other tables. Because of rounding, details may not add to totals.

[1] Some 214 institutions did not report the racial/ethnic status of their student body. Data for 195 of these nonreporting institutions, representing about 5 percent of total enrollment, were imputed. For those institutions which reported race data in 1982, data have been estimated by applying their 1982 race distribution to their total enrollment reported in 1984.

A-4 ACE/UCLA Cooperative Institutional Research Program: Fall 1976
Weighted National Norms for All Freshmen

	All Institutions	All Two-year Colleges	All Four-year Colleges	All Universities	Predominantly Black Colleges	Two-year Colleges Public	Two-year Colleges Private	Four-year Colleges Public	Four-year Private Nonsect.	Four-year Protestant	Four-year Catholic	Universities Public	Universities Private	Predominantly Black Colleges Public	Predominantly Black Colleges Private
Objectives considered to be essential or very important															
achieve in a performing art	11.6	10.0	13.3	11.9	17.7	9.9	10.5	12.8	14.6	14.1	12.5	11.2	14.4	18.1	17.0
be an authority in my field	70.1	68.5	70.6	72.5	78.0	68.5	68.4	70.8	71.2	69.2	71.2	71.9	74.5	76.1	81.8
obtain recognition from colleagues	45.9	44.4	46.1	48.5	59.6	44.6	42.2	46.9	46.7	41.5	48.1	47.1	53.3	58.2	62.6
influence political structure	15.2	13.0	16.6	17.2	25.5	13.2	11.7	15.6	18.6	16.1	18.5	15.9	21.9	24.5	27.6
influence social values	29.7	27.7	32.6	29.2	40.6	27.5	30.3	30.3	35.0	36.1	34.6	28.1	33.1	38.4	45.3
raise a family	57.2	57.2	58.3	55.3	53.1	56.9	59.9	56.9	57.9	62.0	60.9	54.9	56.9	52.4	54.4
have administrative responsibility	31.9	33.8	30.5	30.6	42.6	33.8	33.5	31.4	28.7	28.3	32.7	30.3	31.5	42.9	42.1
be very well off financially	53.1	56.9	49.2	51.7	68.0	57.4	50.9	52.7	46.4	41.5	49.0	51.2	53.3	68.0	68.2
help others in difficulty	63.1	60.0	67.2	62.9	73.4	59.4	66.7	65.4	66.6	70.9	71.9	61.8	66.7	71.1	78.1
theoretical contribution to science	14.0	12.6	13.7	17.1	20.9	12.9	8.9	13.7	15.4	11.5	13.3	16.0	21.0	19.0	24.9
write original works	12.6	10.6	14.3	13.9	16.4	10.6	10.7	14.0	15.7	13.9	14.0	13.1	16.9	15.7	18.0
create artistic work	14.3	14.1	14.5	14.3	16.6	14.0	15.5	14.2	16.2	13.9	13.5	14.3	14.1	17.3	15.4
be successful in my own business	45.0	47.4	42.5	44.5	59.4	47.4	46.5	42.0	44.3	41.9	42.5	44.5	44.4	59.6	59.1
be involved in environmental cleanup	27.7	27.2	28.1	28.2	32.7	27.4	25.8	28.2	30.0	26.4	25.9	28.4	27.2	33.1	32.0
develop philosophy of life	60.8	54.9	65.0	65.8	65.9	54.6	58.9	62.3	68.6	67.7	68.5	64.5	70.6	63.2	71.6
participate in community action	28.8	25.3	32.0	30.7	43.9	24.9	29.4	30.4	33.2	34.5	34.8	30.0	33.1	42.2	47.3
keep up with political affairs	37.4	30.5	40.9	45.4	41.7	30.5	31.4	38.5	45.6	40.6	45.3	43.1	53.6	39.6	46.0
Political orientation															
far left	2.2	2.6	2.0	1.7	5.1	2.6	2.3	2.2	1.9	1.7	1.4	1.6	2.2	5.6	4.2
liberal	25.6	23.3	26.3	29.2	30.1	23.6	19.5	26.6	29.0	22.1	26.4	27.7	34.6	26.5	38.0
middle-of-the-road	56.0	59.4	53.9	52.6	49.0	59.3	61.0	55.5	48.7	53.6	56.2	54.7	45.1	50.4	45.9
conservative	15.2	13.6	16.8	15.8	12.2	13.4	16.2	14.6	19.4	21.5	15.2	15.4	17.3	13.2	10.0
far right	1.0	1.1	1.0	0.7	3.6	1.1	1.0	1.0	0.9	1.1	0.8	0.6	0.9	4.4	2.0
Agree strongly or somewhat															
government not controlling pollution	82.4	81.5	82.6	83.6	78.4	81.6	80.2	82.8	83.2	81.3	82.7	83.5	84.1	77.1	81.1
government not protecting consumer	73.7	74.6	73.2	72.8	76.4	74.8	72.9	74.0	72.9	70.8	73.5	72.5	73.6	75.8	77.9
government should help private colleges	64.7	65.8	66.9	58.8	72.2	64.7	79.6	57.9	74.8	77.1	84.8	54.3	74.5	65.5	86.4

(Continued)

Appendix Table A-4. Continued

	All Institutions	All Two-year Colleges	All Four-year Colleges	All Universities	Predominantly Black Colleges	Two-year Colleges		Four-year Colleges				Universities		Predominantly Black Colleges	
						Public	Private	Public	Private Nonsect.	Protestant	Catholic	Public	Private	Public	Private
federal government discourage energy use	79.7	78.4	80.3	81.2	74.4	78.3	79.5	80.1	80.6	80.1	81.3	80.9	82.1	73.2	76.9
too many rights for criminals	59.7	61.7	58.5	57.6	45.3	61.7	61.9	58.5	57.6	60.6	57.1	58.6	54.4	46.7	42.3
not obey laws against own views	31.9	33.5	31.2	30.1	38.4	33.7	30.3	30.9	31.9	30.9	31.5	29.5	32.4	39.7	35.4
people should be paid equally	26.3	30.9	24.3	20.3	46.2	30.9	31.2	26.2	21.2	22.3	23.2	20.5	19.8	49.8	38.6
grading in high school too easy	57.7	54.4	59.3	61.8	38.5	54.5	54.0	58.4	61.5	61.1	56.0	62.4	60.0	36.0	43.9
women's activities best in home	28.4	31.4	28.3	22.7	35.5	31.5	30.9	27.5	28.0	33.1	25.7	23.0	21.7	38.2	29.7
live together before marriage	48.8	51.5	44.6	50.0	50.0	52.3	42.1	48.9	46.3	31.2	39.5	49.5	51.6	49.2	51.8
discourage large families	55.1	53.3	54.2	59.9	40.5	53.4	52.0	54.3	58.3	56.6	40.3	60.2	58.9	42.3	36.7
sex OK if people like each other	49.4	52.8	44.4	50.5	53.2	53.8	40.3	49.2	45.9	31.6	36.1	49.6	53.5	53.1	53.4
women should get job equality	92.0	90.4	92.7	94.3	90.5	90.3	91.5	93.0	92.8	91.0	93.7	94.2	94.5	89.6	92.4
wealthy should pay more taxes	76.2	77.3	75.5	75.0	76.8	77.5	74.6	77.1	73.3	73.4	74.6	75.6	72.9	75.2	80.1
marijuana should be legalized	48.9	51.1	45.2	50.7	49.8	51.8	41.4	49.1	45.5	32.0	45.4	50.2	52.4	48.4	52.9
busing OK to achieve balance	37.0	39.8	36.3	32.3	69.5	39.7	41.3	37.8	34.2	34.3	35.2	31.5	35.2	70.6	67.2
can do little to change society	44.3	47.1	42.4	41.9	45.8	47.4	43.1	44.8	40.3	38.8	40.1	42.3	40.7	47.5	42.2
prohibit homosexual relations	47.0	51.7	46.6	38.5	52.1	51.4	55.3	45.1	43.7	56.7	43.8	39.7	34.4	54.4	47.3
college regulate students off campus	14.0	15.0	14.9	10.8	28.0	14.8	17.2	13.3	16.0	20.1	12.1	10.4	12.1	30.1	23.5
students appreciate college more if pay more	47.4	44.7	48.5	51.0	37.1	44.3	49.2	46.0	50.3	53.0	51.4	51.3	50.1	37.3	36.9
students help evaluate faculty	71.4	68.9	71.9	75.7	63.8	69.0	68.1	71.9	73.2	70.4	71.5	75.6	76.1	62.0	67.7
abolish college grades	21.0	23.0	20.4	17.9	27.6	23.2	21.3	21.1	19.8	19.4	19.7	17.9	17.8	29.6	23.2
deemphasize organized sports	26.8	26.8	26.8	26.7	31.4	26.9	25.8	25.6	29.2	27.9	26.4	26.0	29.2	33.4	27.1
regulate student publications	34.0	38.7	34.0	24.9	52.7	38.2	45.3	32.2	32.0	42.5	33.8	25.6	22.4	56.2	45.1
college has right to ban speaker	25.2	27.7	25.5	19.8	31.0	27.5	31.0	24.3	24.9	31.3	23.1	19.8	19.8	33.3	26.3
preferential treatment for disadvantaged	37.0	41.0	36.3	30.3	58.0	40.7	43.7	37.3	33.5	38.4	32.6	31.0	27.9	58.4	57.2
adopt open admissions at public colleges	34.7	43.9	29.8	24.4	46.7	44.5	36.4	30.4	26.9	30.9	31.0	24.9	22.7	48.4	43.0
use same degree standard for all	76.7	76.2	76.5	77.7	73.0	76.5	72.6	76.5	76.6	76.9	75.8	77.5	78.1	72.3	74.4
students have right to ban speakers	57.7	56.6	58.0	59.7	60.0	57.0	51.7	59.0	58.6	53.5	59.2	59.0	62.1	59.0	62.2

Source: Astin et al., *The American Freshman, Fall 1976*, pp. 47, 55, and 60.

A-5 Weighted National Norms for All Freshmen: Fall 1986

	All Institutions	All Two-year Colleges	All Four-year Colleges	All Universities	Predominantly Black Colleges	Two-year Colleges		Four-year Colleges				Universities		Predominantly Black Colleges	
						Public	Private	Public	Private Nonsect.	Protestant	Catholic	Public	Private	Public	Private
Objectives considered to be essential or very important															
achieve in a performing art	10.5	7.9	12.3	11.5	14.1	7.3	12.2	11.1	15.7	12.8	10.7	10.6	14.3	14.7	12.8
become authority in my field	71.8	68.5	73.0	74.8	79.9	68.1	70.9	73.9	72.2	71.1	72.5	74.9	74.4	77.7	83.9
obtain recognition from colleagues	54.7	50.8	56.0	58.2	63.5	50.3	54.4	57.1	55.6	52.3	56.3	58.4	57.5	60.9	68.4
influence political structure	14.5	11.2	16.3	16.6	25.9	10.9	13.6	15.4	18.0	16.0	17.7	15.7	19.8	24.7	28.0
influence social values	32.5	29.2	35.5	32.2	45.1	28.3	36.1	33.6	38.3	38.0	37.1	31.4	35.0	43.9	47.4
raise a family	67.0	64.7	68.2	68.6	58.7	64.3	67.9	67.3	68.0	70.7	70.8	67.4	72.5	56.5	62.9
have administrative responsibility	44.2	43.1	44.7	45.1	52.4	43.0	43.9	46.6	41.5	41.1	47.0	45.8	42.7	51.7	53.8
be very well off financially	73.2	75.4	71.1	73.2	85.6	75.6	73.4	73.9	68.1	65.3	71.0	74.5	68.5	84.9	87.1
help others in difficulty	57.2	53.8	60.7	56.5	71.4	52.6	62.4	59.4	62.3	63.0	61.6	55.5	60.2	69.2	75.5
theoretical contribution to science	12.6	10.5	12.2	16.3	17.3	10.7	9.1	12.3	13.5	10.4	10.9	16.2	16.9	15.7	20.6
write original works	11.3	8.1	12.9	13.2	14.0	7.9	10.0	11.9	16.2	12.6	12.0	12.3	16.1	13.9	14.1
create artistic work	10.9	9.3	11.9	11.7	11.9	8.7	14.3	10.5	17.0	10.6	10.8	11.7	11.9	12.6	10.5
be successful in own business	49.0	50.1	48.3	48.5	65.1	49.2	56.5	47.8	49.7	46.7	51.1	49.4	45.4	63.5	67.9
be involved in environmental cleanup	15.9	16.3	16.2	15.0	25.3	16.0	18.2	16.0	17.9	15.5	14.5	15.2	14.4	24.9	25.9
develop philosophy of life	40.6	34.6	43.6	44.6	56.4	33.6	42.0	41.3	48.6	45.2	42.9	42.8	50.8	53.1	62.6
participate in community action	18.5	15.1	20.9	19.6	34.3	14.3	20.8	19.8	22.5	22.2	21.7	19.0	21.6	31.4	39.9
promote racial understanding	27.2	22.1	31.1	28.4	62.9	21.3	28.3	29.5	35.7	31.1	30.3	26.8	33.9	58.7	70.8
be expert on finance/commerce	25.2	23.0	26.3	26.7	41.4	22.8	24.0	27.3	24.4	23.9	29.0	26.7	26.6	41.6	41.1
Political orientation															
far left	2.0	2.2	2.0	1.7	3.6	2.2	2.4	1.9	2.2	2.0	1.6	1.7	1.7	3.7	3.5
liberal	22.0	19.4	22.9	24.1	29.1	19.2	21.0	21.9	26.6	21.8	22.4	23.7	25.5	26.2	34.6
middle-of-the-road	56.0	61.6	53.8	51.4	48.2	62.0	59.0	56.6	48.4	50.7	54.6	53.4	44.7	50.1	44.5
conservative	18.7	15.3	20.0	21.6	17.1	15.2	16.3	18.3	21.3	24.0	20.3	20.1	26.8	17.5	16.4
far right	1.3	1.4	1.3	1.2	2.0	1.4	1.3	1.3	1.4	1.5	1.0	1.2	1.3	2.5	1.1

(Continued)

Appendix Table A-5, Continued

	All Institutions	All Two-year Colleges	All Four-year Colleges	All Universities	Predominantly Black Colleges	Two-year Colleges		Four-year Colleges				Universities		Predominantly Black Colleges	
						Public	Private	Public	Private Nonsect.	Protestant	Catholic	Public	Private	Public	Private
Agree strongly or somewhat															
government not protecting consumer	62.8	66.6	63.0	57.0	74.2	66.6	66.4	63.7	62.3	62.2	61.8	58.0	53.8	74.4	73.9
government not promoting disarmament	66.0	64.6	67.0	66.3	75.9	65.0	62.0	65.6	69.6	66.6	70.4	65.7	68.4	74.6	78.4
government not controlling pollution	78.0	77.3	78.6	78.0	78.1	77.4	76.3	78.0	80.5	78.2	78.2	77.7	79.1	76.9	80.4
government discourage energy use	69.7	68.3	70.7	70.2	69.8	68.4	67.1	70.9	71.6	69.2	69.9	70.2	70.1	69.2	70.9
raise taxes to reduce deficit	23.2	19.7	24.0	27.1	21.4	19.6	20.5	23.4	25.4	25.0	22.8	26.7	28.5	23.1	18.1
increase federal military spending	26.9	28.1	27.1	24.9	27.7	27.9	29.8	29.3	23.9	26.2	22.0	25.7	22.4	31.2	20.9
nuclear disarmament attainable	54.6	54.3	55.4	53.7	53.4	54.4	53.7	55.3	55.8	54.5	57.2	54.0	52.9	52.4	55.2
abolish death penalty	25.4	24.5	27.2	24.0	43.9	24.2	26.9	25.8	29.2	26.9	31.8	22.8	28.3	45.4	41.1
need national health care plan	62.1	67.1	62.0	55.3	75.3	67.0	67.4	62.5	62.6	58.9	62.1	55.8	53.8	75.8	74.2
abortion should be legalized	58.6	55.6	58.1	64.0	59.7	55.9	52.9	60.4	60.1	52.8	46.4	65.8	57.9	56.3	66.0
high school grading too easy	48.7	45.7	48.7	53.3	36.3	46.2	42.0	47.0	50.8	51.3	49.5	52.2	56.9	35.5	37.8
women's activities best in home	20.3	22.4	20.4	17.3	29.4	22.3	23.2	20.7	19.6	20.6	19.7	17.2	17.7	33.1	22.6
live together before marriage	51.1	54.4	48.0	51.5	51.5	55.3	47.3	50.4	49.0	39.7	43.7	52.9	46.7	52.4	49.8
women should get job equality	92.0	90.5	92.4	93.7	90.5	90.4	90.8	92.3	92.6	92.4	92.6	93.6	94.0	89.0	93.3
wealthy should pay more taxes	72.1	73.8	72.3	69.4	74.1	74.5	68.4	74.3	69.5	70.5	69.1	70.3	66.3	73.1	75.9
marijuana should be legalized	21.3	22.3	20.2	21.9	21.0	22.4	21.2	20.7	21.8	16.6	18.9	22.7	19.2	22.5	18.3
busing OK to achieve balance	56.1	59.4	56.3	51.2	70.2	59.2	60.8	55.9	57.7	55.6	56.1	51.4	50.5	69.7	71.3
prohibit homosexual relations	52.2	58.4	51.4	44.5	58.7	58.1	60.6	52.4	47.8	55.0	47.9	45.6	40.5	60.0	56.2
colleges regulate students off-campus	12.4	13.3	13.1	10.0	24.5	13.1	14.6	12.9	13.8	13.6	10.9	9.4	11.9	27.1	19.6
students help evaluate faculty	70.3	66.1	70.8	75.5	65.3	66.4	63.8	69.9	72.6	71.1	71.6	75.1	76.9	63.9	67.9
college has right to ban speaker	25.6	28.3	25.2	22.3	30.9	28.1	30.4	25.5	24.5	25.5	24.9	22.3	22.1	33.0	27.1
college divest S. Africa invest	46.9	42.4	48.0	51.6	51.6	42.9	38.6	46.5	52.9	46.5	47.5	50.2	56.3	47.3	59.5
college increases earning power	70.7	77.1	68.3	65.5	79.2	77.7	72.5	71.9	62.1	64.7	66.4	68.3	56.0	80.1	77.6

Source: Astin et al., The American Freshman, Fall 1986, p. 64.

A-6 Percentage of Graduates of Two-Year Programs Who Enter Four-Year Programs: 1980, 1984, 1985

Institutions	Institutions In Universe[1]	Institutions Number in Table	Institutions Percentage of Universe	Years 1980	Years 1984	Years 1985	Difference in Percentage from 1980–1985	Difference in Percentage from 1984–1985
Four year public								
Doctoral-granting	69	12	17	41.4	41.8	41.9	0.4	0.1
Other public	163	66	40	42.2	44.9	45.4	3.2	0.5
All four-year public	232	78	34	42.0	43.8	44.2	2.2	0.4
Four-year private								
Doctoral-granting	40	8	20	87.1	88.1	87.9	0.7	−0.3
Liberal arts	34	10	29	62.5	66.5	65.8	3.3	−0.8
Other private I	155	66	43	62.5	62.3	61.1	−1.4	−1.2
Other private II	146	60	41	57.6	56.5	56.3	−1.3	−0.2
Special purpose	110	50	45	41.8	39.9	40.2	−1.6	0.4
All four-year private	485	194	40	62.9	62.7	61.9	−1.1	−0.8
All four-year institutions	717	272	38	50.7	51.9	51.7	1.0	−0.2
Two-year public								
Community	796	608	76	42.3	42.6	42.1	−0.1	−0.5
Technical	128	93	73	16.2	15.3	15.0	−1.1	−0.3
All two-year public	924	701	76	40.6	40.7	40.2	−0.3	−0.5
Two-year private								
All two-year private	297	168	57	40.7	39.4	40.3	−0.4	0.9
All two-year institutions	1221	869	71	40.6	40.7	40.2	−0.3	−0.4

1 Universe includes only institutions that award associate degrees. Reprinted by permission from *Summary Statistics: Annual Survey of Colleges, 1986–87*, table 43, p. 90, copyright © 1986 by College Entrance Examination Board, New York.

A-7 Percentage[1] of Two- and Four-Year College Entrants Who Had Persisted, Transferred, Completed Short-Term Programs, or Withdrawn, by Selected Student Characteristics: February 1982.

Characteristics[2]	Four-year College			Two-year College		
	Persister	Transfer[3]	Completer/Withdrawer[3]	Persister	Transfer[4]	Completer/Withdrawer[2]
All students	75	15[3]	10	59	16[4]	26
Racial/ethnic group:						
Hispanic	66	17	17	65	11	24
Black	71	14	15	61	15	24
White	75	15	9	57	16	27
Asian American	86[5]	12	2	70[5]	21	9
American Indian	81	11	9	61	21	18
Socioeconomic status (SES):						
High	77	17	7	59	21	20
Middle	75	14	11	59	15	26
Low	71	14	15	59	10	31
High-school program:						
Academic	79	15	7	60	23	16
General	66	18	17	56	12	32
Vocational/technical	64	16	20	62	9	29

Note: Sample includes some persons who completed short-term programs. The survey instruments did not contain the information required to distinguish between these two categories.

1 Percentages are based on those individuals who entered college before June 1981.

2 Students who had completed short-term programs (i.e., completers) and students who had left school without completing programs (i.e., withdrawers) were not differentiated in this table because the information needed for so doing was not available in the HS&B first follow-up survey.

3 Includes 10 percent four- to four-year college transfers and 5 percent four- to two-year college transfers.

4 Includes 8 percent two- to two-year college transfers and 8 percent two- to four-year college transfers.

5 The apparently higher persistence of Asian Americans is based on a small sample of Asian Americans and does not differ significantly from the rate for whites.

Source: CES, *High School and Beyond, Two Years After High School: A Capsule Description of 1980 Seniors*, table 4, p. 9.

A-8

Associate Degrees Conferred in Institutions of Higher Education, by Sex and Field of Study: 50 States and District of Columbia, Academic Years 1983–1985

Field of Study[1]	1983			1984			1985		
	Total	Men	Women	Total	Men	Women	Total	Men	Women
Total	456,441	207,141	249,300	452,416	202,762	249,654	454,712	202,932	251,780
Agriculture and natural resources, total	7,760	5,228	2,532	6,879	4,763	2,116	6,554	4,459	2,095
Agricultural business and agricultural production	4,779	3,397	1,382	4,395	3,140	1,255	4,175	2,990	1,185
Agricultural science	1,506	660	846	1,367	706	661	1,393	665	728
Renewable natural resources	1,475	1,171	304	1,117	917	200	986	804	182
Architecture and environmental design	1,689	333	1,356	1,495	258	1,237	1,490	274	1,216
Area and ethnic studies	23	10	13	30	11	19	32	8	24
Business and management	120,236	44,018	76,218	120,034	42,494	77,540	120,731	41,319	79,412
Accounting	6,146	1,968	4,178	6,128	1,940	4,188	5,527	1,806	3,721
Business and management, general	13,956	6,725	7,231	13,934	6,561	7,373	12,887	5,782	7,105
Business administration and management	19,717	9,877	9,840	18,683	9,047	9,636	19,530	8,963	10,567
Business and management, other	11,711	7,028	4,683	11,424	6,464	4,960	11,307	6,462	4,845
Business data processing	16,307	7,307	9,000	18,709	8,419	10,290	18,835	8,518	10,317
Secretarial and related programs	20,830	235	20,595	21,070	309	20,761	21,845	373	21,472
Business and office, other	15,079	5,396	9,683	14,082	4,731	9,351	14,378	4,454	9,924
Marketing and distribution	15,622	5,113	10,509	15,214	4,630	10,584	15,624	4,559	11,065
Consumer and personal services	868	369	499	790	393	397	798	402	396

1 Major fields of study appear flush left. Miscellaneous subgroupings under fields are in roman type.

(Continued)

Appendix Table A-8, Continued

Field of Study[1]	1983			1984			1985		
	Total	Men	Women	Total	Men	Women	Total	Men	Women
Communications	2,049	1,023	1,026	1,881	1,012	869	1,846	997	849
Communications technologies	1,821	1,100	721	1,871	1,109	762	2,270	1,483	787
Computer and information sciences	10,065	4,996	5,069	12,824	6,492	6,332	12,677	6,519	6,158
Education	7,653	2,393	5,260	7,652	2,221	5,431	7,580	2,340	5,240
Engineering	3,699	3,313	386	4,459	3,980	479	3,881	3,473	408
Engineering technologies	58,898	53,576	5,322	57,735	52,776	4,959	59,951	54,888	5,063
Mechanics and repairers	9,177	8,780	397	9,253	8,789	464	8,666	8,265	401
Construction trades	2,407	2,231	176	2,179	2,102	77	2,341	2,261	80
Engineering technologies, other	47,314	42,565	4,749	46,303	41,885	4,418	48,944	44,362	4,582
Foreign languages	355	168	187	326	148	178	388	195	193
Health sciences	66,448	7,725	58,723	68,270	7,971	60,299	68,453	8,106	60,347
Dental assisting	4,560	407	4,153	4,389	373	4,016	4,160	352	3,808
Emergency medical technician ambulance	500	357	143	139	78	61	74	47	27
Emergency medical technician paramedic	201	139	62	186	125	61	211	144	67
Medical lab technician	2,712	478	2,234	3,037	545	2,492	2,788	501	2,287
Medical assisting	1,835	33	1,802	1,932	32	1,900	2,196	58	2,138
Nursing assisting	97	21	76	140	21	119	133	21	112
Practical nursing	1,622	118	1,504	1,389	96	1,293	1,252	93	1,159
Nursing, general	37,395	2,529	34,866	40,114	2,977	37,137	40,334	3,072	37,262
Health sciences, other	17,526	3,643	13,883	16,944	3,724	13,220	17,305	3,818	13,487
Home economics	9,369	2,303	7,066	9,247	2,420	6,827	9,611	2,622	6,989
Law	1,742	267	1,475	1,813	302	1,511	2,060	311	1,749
Letters	638	233	405	630	219	411	617	202	415
Liberal/general studies	109,619	49,365	60,254	108,019	48,557	59,462	106,396	47,177	59,219
Library and archival sciences	218	29	189	155	23	132	128	16	112
Life sciences	1,109	548	561	1,209	554	655	1,121	521	600

Field									
Mathematics	809	502	307	783	496	287	789	489	300
Military sciences	88	86	2	87	83	4	23	23	0
Multi/interdisciplinary studies	10,339	4,767	5,572	8,218	3,702	4,516	8,525	3,910	4,615
Parks and recreation	1,022	466	556	731	351	380	728	352	376
Philosophy and religion	193	117	76	144	95	49	138	99	39
Theology	677	372	305	712	403	309	701	398	303
Physical sciences	3,142	2,046	1,096	2,877	1,888	989	2,193	1,384	809
Science technologies	1,438	911	527	1,369	875	494	1,138	684	456
Physical sciences, other	1,704	1,135	569	1,508	1,013	495	1,055	700	355
Psychology	1,031	363	668	1,088	360	728	983	312	671
Protective services	13,163	9,950	3,213	11,983	8,931	3,052	12,305	9,168	3,137
Criminal justice administration and studies	5,996	4,289	1,707	5,666	3,978	1,688	5,533	3,848	1,685
Law enforcement and security services	4,074	3,007	1,067	4,019	3,000	1,019	4,211	3,148	1,063
Fire control and safety	2,150	2,072	78	1,671	1,612	59	1,724	1,661	63
Protective services, other	943	582	361	627	341	286	837	511	326
Public affairs	4,344	1,822	2,522	4,027	1,744	2,283	3,675	1,705	1,970
Social sciences	2,958	1,385	1,573	2,734	1,174	1,560	2,587	1,105	1,482
Visual and performing arts	15,284	8,637	6,647	14,503	8,225	6,278	13,742	8,052	5,690
Fine arts, general	1,422	537	885	1,074	363	711	1,033	386	647
Graphic arts technician	2,131	619	1,512	1,972	513	1,459	1,686	505	1,181
Precision production	8,691	6,176	2,515	9,166	6,329	2,837	8,711	6,081	2,630
Visual and performing arts, other	3,040	1,305	1,735	2,291	1,020	1,271	2,312	1,080	1,232

Note: At the associate degree level, data were imputed by field of study for 103 institutions for 1983 and for 23 institutions for 1984 which did not report data. Data for the 18 nonrespondents in 1985 were imputed at the total levels only, so field-of-study data do not add to grand totals by 2,537 (total), 1,025 (men), and 1,512 (women).

Source: CES, Unpublished tabulations from Associate Degrees and Other Awards Below the Baccalaureate, 1983 to 1985, table 1.1, p. 35.

A-9 Current-Fund Revenues of Two-Year and Four-Year Institutions: 1975–76 (in Thousands of Dollars)

Source	Two-Year Institutions	Four-Year Institutions
Tuition & fees	849,796	6,986,574
Federal appropriations	117,665	779,986
State appropriations	2,093,354	8,409,109
Local appropriations	1,170,265	252,247
Federal grants, unrestricted	21,004	547,002
Federal grants, restricted	271,304	3,195,101
State grants, restricted	14,414	39,113
State grants, unrestricted	61,144	359,758
Local grants, unrestricted	4,229	13,515
Local grants, restricted	12,589	154,215
Private gifts, unrestricted	420,289	743,481
Private gifts, restricted	17,571	1,022,293
Endowment income, unrestricted	6,439	350,637
Endowment income, restricted	868	3,057,383
Sales and services of educational activities	20,784	560,563
Sales and services of auxiliary activities	343,908	3,953,902
Sales and services of hospital	0.00	2,083,825
Other sources	108,261	696,671
Independent operations	76	8,888,534
Total current-fund revenue	5,155,697	31,342,581

Source: ACE, Department of Policy Analysis and Research tabulations on Higher Education General Information surveys, 1975–76.

Current-Fund Revenues of Two-Year and Four-Year Institutions: 1984–85 (in Thousands of Dollars)

Source	Two-Year Institutions	Four-Year Institutions
Tuition & fees	2,501,338	18,974,865
Federal appropriations	80,732	1,551,606
State appropriations	4,916,244	21,685,352
Local appropriations	1,812,504	180,787
Federal grants, unrestricted	21,207	1,454,724
Federal grants, restricted	1,156,662	7,785,874
State grants, unrestricted	26,035	113,302
State grants, restricted	255,773	837,233
Local grants, unrestricted	19,734	44,548
Local grant, restricted	37,908	314,053
Private gifts, unrestricted	65,552	1,880,506
Private gifts, restricted	56,008	2,901,178
Endowment income, unrestricted	23,329	1,205,441
Endowment income, restricted	6,526	862,245
Sales and services of educational activities	57,102	2,081,272
Sales and services of auxiliary activities	820,385	9,295,095
Sales and services of hospital	0.00	7,474,575
Other sources	348,695	2,681,837
Independent operations	11,654	1,882,708
Total current-fund revenue	12,217,387	83,207,200

Source: ACE, Department of Policy Analysis and Research tabulations based on Higher Education General Information surveys, 1984–85.

A-11 Current-Fund Revenues of Two-Year Institutions by Control: 1984–85 (in Thousands of Dollars)

Source	Public	Private
Tuition & fees	1,800,087	701,251
Federal appropriations	76,763	3,967
State appropriations	4,893,596	22,648
Local appropriations	1,807,920	4,583
Federal grants, unrestricted	17,538	3,669
Federal grants, restricted	979,237	177,425
State grants, unrestricted	24,410	1,625
State grants, restricted	240,282	15,490
Local grants, unrestricted	19,547	187
Local grants, restricted	37,271	637
Private gifts, unrestricted	100,889	55,463
Private gifts, restricted	47,533	8,474
Endowment income, unrestricted	10,348	12,980
Endowment income, restricted	2,529	3,996
State and services of educational activities	4,759	9,563
Sales and services of auxiliary activities	689,367	131,018
Other sources	3,161,190	32,576
Independent operations	11,355	299
Total Current-fund revenue	11,031,533	1,185,854

Source: ACE, Department of Policy Analysis and Research tabulations based on Higher Education General Information surveys, 1984–85.

	1986	1985	% Change
Federal Funding			
All colleges	7.4	8.8	−15.9
Public only	6.9	8.3	−16.9
single campus	6.9	8.2	−15.9
district	8.6	9.4	−8.5
State Funding			
All colleges	48.9	48.3	1.2
Public only	49.2	48.5	1.4
single campus	51.5	50.8	1.4
district	40.8	39.8	2.5
Local Funding			
All colleges	23.4	23.1	1.3
Public only	23.5	23.2	1.3
single campus	21.9	21.7	0.9
district	28.2	28.4	−0.7
Tuition Revenues			
All colleges	17.4	16.4	6.1
Public only	17.5	16.4	6.7
single campus	17.6	17.0	3.5
district	17.4	15.8	10.1

	1986–87	1985–86	% Change
Average Budget			
All colleges	12,918,592	12,275,995	5.2
Public only	12,987,210	12,336,784	5.3
single campus	10,390,782	9,856,478	5.4
district	23,519,236	22,014,781	6.8

Source: *Supplement to the AACJC Letter,* no. 246, June 16, 1987.

A-13

Current-Fund Expenditures and Expenditures per Full-Time-Equivalent Student in Institutions of Higher Education, by Type and Control of Institution: United States, 1970–71 to 1984–85

Control of Institution and Year	All Institutions			Four-Year Institutions			Two-Year Institutions		
	Current Dollars	Current-Fund Expenditures, Constant 1984–85 Dollars[1] in Millions	Current-Fund Expenditures Per Student, in Constant 1984–85 Dollars	Current Dollars	Current-Fund Expenditures, Constant 1984–85 Dollars[1] in Millions	Current-Fund Expenditures per Student, in Constant 1984–85 Dollars	Current Dollars	Current-Fund Expenditures, Constant 1984–85 Dollars[1] in Millions	Current-fund Expenditures per Student, in Constant 1984–85 Dollars
All institutions									
1970–71	$23,375	$63,128	$9,369	$21,049	$56,844	$10,890	$2,327	$6,283	$4,139
1971–72	25,560	65,367	9,144	22,851	58,439	10,763	2,709	6,928	4,030
1972–73	27,956	67,895	9,360	24,653	59,874	11,074	3,303	8,021	4,343
1973–74	30,714	69,672	9,348	26,912	61,049	11,092	3,802	8,624	4,423
1974–75	35,058	73,258	9,385	30,596	63,936	11,404	4,461	9,322	4,239
1975–76	38,903	76,248	8,992	33,811	66,268	11,231	5,092	9,980	3,869
1976–77	42,600	78,404	9,432	37,052	68,193	11,661	5,548	10,211	4,143
1977–78	45,971	79,313	9,425	39,899	68,836	11,598	6,072	10,476	4,224
1978–79	50,721	81,214	9,728	44,163	70,714	11,920	6,558	10,501	4,346
1979–80	56,914	82,981	9,777	49,661	72,406	12,035	7,253	10,575	4,279
1980–81	64,053	84,296	9,558	55,840	73,488	11,927	8,212	10,808	4,067
1981–82	70,339	84,122	9,332	61,333	73,351	11,736	9,006	10,771	3,896
1982–83	75,936	85,403	9,394	66,238	74,497	11,922	9,697	10,906	3,837
1983–84[2]	81,993	87,512	9,554	71,680	76,504	12,098	10,314	11,008	3,882
1984–85[2]	89,951	89,951	10,056	78,744	78,744	12,516	11,207	11,207	4,219
Public institutions									
1970–71	14,996	40,499	8,176	12,899	34,835	9,839	2,097	5,664	4,009
1971–72	16,484	42,158	7,888	14,014	35,840	9,606	2,470	6,318	3,916
1972–73	18,204	44,211	8,108	15,146	36,785	9,925	3,058	7,426	4,252
1973–74	20,336	46,132	8,195	16,802	38,114	10,072	3,534	8,017	4,345
1974–75	23,490	49,086	8,257	19,309	40,349	10,487	4,181	8,736	4,166
1975–76	26,184	51,319	7,868	21,392	41,927	10,336	4,792	9,392	3,809
1976–77	28,635	52,702	8,300	23,411	43,087	10,776	5,224	9,615	4,089
1977–78	30,725	53,010	8,287	25,013	43,155	10,684	5,712	9,855	4,180

1978–79	33,733	54,013	8,602	27,600	44,194	11,059	6,132	9,819	4,301
1979–80	37,768	55,066	8,614	30,979	45,168	11,127	6,789	9,899	4,242
1980–81	42,280	55,641	8,377	34,677	45,636	10,975	7,602	10,005	4,028
1981–82	46,219	55,275	8,151	37,890	45,313	10,767	8,330	9,962	3,872
1982–83	49,573	55,753	8,138	40,616	45,680	10,823	8,957	10,074	3,830
1983–84	53,087	56,659	8,234	43,588	46,522	10,906	9,499	10,138	3,875
1984–85[2]	58,314	58,314	8,721	48,017	48,017	11,330	10,297	10,297	4,201
Independent Institutions									
1970–71	8,379	22,629	12,680	8,150	22,009	13,106	230	620	5,883
1971–72	9,075	23,209	12,864	8,837	22,599	13,304	239	610	5,780
1972–73	9,752	23,684	13,151	9,507	23,089	13,577	245	595	5,931
1973–74	10,377	23,540	12,907	10,110	22,934	13,337	267	606	5,810
1974–75	11,568	24,172	12,991	11,287	23,586	13,411	280	586	5,746
1975–76	12,719	24,929	12,736	12,419	24,341	13,201	300	588	5,179
1976–77	13,965	25,702	13,096	13,641	25,106	13,574	324	597	5,278
1977–78	15,246	26,303	13,029	14,885	25,682	13,545	360	621	5,058
1978–79	16,988	27,201	13,145	16,563	26,520	13,695	425	681	5,129
1979–80	19,146	27,915	13,326	18,682	27,238	13,920	464	676	4,903
1980–81	21,773	28,654	13,164	21,163	27,851	13,904	610	803	4,625
1981–82	24,120	28,846	12,917	23,444	28,038	13,735	676	809	4,215
1982–83	26,363	29,650	13,230	25,623	28,817	14,208	740	832	3,912
1983–84[2]	28,907	30,852	13,545	28,092	29,982	14,568	815	870	3,959
1984–85[2]	31,637	31,637	14,007	30,727	30,727	14,963	910	910	4,433

Note: Because of rounding, details may not add to totals.

1 Dollars adjusted by the higher education price index.

2 Expenditure-per-student calculation includes only those institutions for which both finance and enrollment data were available.

Source: *Digest of Education Statistics, 1987*, table 205, p. 235.

Position	Title	Median	First Quartile	Third Quartile	Number of Institution
1.0	Chief Executive Officer, System	$75,000	$62,515	$84,163	53
2.0	Chief Executive Officer, Single Institution	$62,441	$55,680	$69,865	377
3.0	Executive Vice President	$53,000	$47,000	$62,400	86
4.0	Chief Academic Officer	$48,695	$42,322	$54,923	392
5.0	Chief Business Officer	$46,721	$40,000	$53,869	404
6.0	Chief Student Affairs Officer	$44,691	$38,904	$51,500	368
7.0	Chief Development Officer	$39,630	$31,350	$45,000	123
8.0	Chief Public Relations Officer	$31,500	$25,000	$40,944	178
9.0	Chief Planning Officer	$44,405	$37,800	$52,631	64
10.0	Chief Personnel/Human Resources Officer	$39,450	$32,889	$50,167	142
11.0	Chief Health Professions Officer	$42,350	$33,186	$50,172	23
12.0	Chief Budgeting Officer	$41,379	$35,126	$48,403	70
13.0	General Counsel	$47,515	$37,000	$59,000	14
14.0	Registrar	$32,386	$24,696	$40,000	245
16.0	Director, Learning Resources Center	$36,876	$30,560	$42,915	226
17.0	Director, Library Services	$33,753	$26,933	$39,477	218
18.0	Director, Computer Center	$38,173	$31,500	$45,430	226
19.0	Director, Computer Center Operations/Academic	$33,079	$28,711	$39,107	38
20.0	Director, Computer Center Operations/Administrative	$34,350	$29,000	$45,464	48
21.0	Director, Educational Media Services	$32,892	$26,047	$37,968	114
22.0	Director, Institutional Research	$36,267	$29,822	$42,167	144
23.0	Director, Special and Deferred Gifts	$30,000	$22,500	$41,920	11
24.0	Administrator, Grants and Contracts	$34,120	$31,427	$41,473	66
25.0	Director, Affirmative Action/Equal Employment	$39,317	$30,318	$42,954	42
26.0	Chaplain	$23,600	$16,728	$27,000	11
27.0	Comptroller	$37,333	$30,739	$44,466	165
28.0	Director, Accounting	$30,800	$24,000	$37,500	128
29.0	Director, Internal Audit	$34,215	$29,172	$40,753	35
30.0	Bursar	$27,941	$20,000	$34,031	44
31.0	Director, Food Services	$25,502	$18,510	$29,945	67
32.0	Chief Physical Plant/Facilities Management Officer	$33,208	$27,250	$40,374	310
33.0	Director, Student Activities	$29,900	$24,004	$36,209	213
34.0	Director, Purchasing	$29,562	$23,936	$35,300	153
35.0	Director, Bookstore	$21,672	$17,004	$27,586	194
36.0	Director, Campus Security	$26,303	$21,053	$31,835	135
37.0	Director, Information Systems	$43,000	$33,281	$50,164	50
38.0	Director, News Bureau	$25,215	$23,112	$28,812	16
39.0	Director, Auxiliary Services	$32,315	$28,477	$43,032	61
40.0	Director, Admissions	$31,836	$26,600	$38,188	185
41.0	Director, Foreign Students	$23,345	$20,525	$26,845	14
42.0	Director, International Studies Education	$38,851	$27,225	$41,400	7
43.0	Director, Student Financial Aid	$30,009	$24,000	$36,000	318
44.0	Director, Student Placement	$28,106	$23,148	$33,900	164
45.0	Director, Student Counseling	$35,391	$29,975	$41,390	229
46.0	Director, Student Union	$33,495	$28,752	$38,297	14

Position	Title	Median	First Quartile	Third Quartile	Number of Institutions
47.0	Director, Student Health Services (Physician Administrator)	$23,210	$22,200	$35,505	5
48.0	Director, Student Health Services (Nurse Administrator)	$23,507	$17,775	$30,105	83
49.0	Director, Student Housing	$23,130	$18,000	$29,578	35
50.0	Director, Athletics	$35,904	$28,872	$43,857	131
51.0	Director, Athletics/Men	$36,000	$30,000	$39,845	6
52.0	Director, Athletics/Women	$27,600	$17,739	$39,845	7
53.0	Director, Campus Recreation/Intramurals	$21,477	$19,234	$24,346	29
54.0	Director, Alumni Affairs	$22,500	$19,138	$28,789	41
55.0	Director, Information Office	$27,354	$22,632	$33,420	90
56.0	Director, Community Services	$34,879	$29,375	$41,751	142
58.0	Director, Publications	$25,596	$21,327	$30,472	30
59.0	Director, Risk Management and Insurance	$33,102	$30,899	$43,163	7
60.0	Chief Planning and Budget Officer	$47,161	$38,100	$52,998	9
61.0	Chief Development and Public Relations Officer	$37,022	$29,500	$43,052	40
62.0	Director, Personnel and Affirmative Action	$33,600	$26,960	$43,163	84
63.0	Director, Admissions and Financial Aid	$35,144	$29,945	$40,565	36
65.0	Director, Development and Alumni Affairs	$33,667	$29,075	$40,944	23
66.0	Director, Admissions and Registrar	$37,914	$31,095	$42,924	102
68.0	Dean, Agriculture	$43,560	$38,187	$47,495	9
69.0	Dean, Arts and Letters	$40,656	$35,944	$43,880	36
70.0	Dean, Arts and Sciences	$43,470	$38,477	$50,400	65
71.0	Dean, Business	$42,050	$36,176	$47,165	147
72.0	Dean, Communications	$43,302	$38,892	$47,456	25
73.0	Dean, Continuing Education	$41,425	$35,010	$46,770	177
75.0	Dean, Education	$39,181	$34,537	$41,636	18
76.0	Dean, Engineering	$44,325	$40,208	$49,050	38
78.0	Dean, Extension	$41,359	$33,000	$49,641	27
79.0	Dean, Fine Arts	$41,328	$37,250	$48,696	31
81.0	Dean, Health Related Professions	$40,613	$36,979	$48,760	79
82.0	Dean, Home Economics	$41,228	$40,000	$46,572	6
83.0	Dean, Humanities	$41,792	$36,570	$48,150	84
84.0	Dean, Instruction	$46,295	$41,105	$51,810	41
86.0	Dean, Library and Information Sciences	$44,859	$36,876	$48,640	16
87.0	Dean, Mathematics	$41,319	$37,927	$46,367	52
89.0	Dean, Music	$46,446	$37,883	$47,844	5
90.0	Dean, Nursing	$38,167	$34,300	$43,115	70
91.0	Dean, Occupation Studies/Vocational Education/Technology	$43,480	$37,927	$49,641	172
94.0	Dean, Sciences	$41,738	$36,005	$49,290	87
95.0	Dean, Social Sciences	$42,540	$37,985	$47,276	86
97.0	Dean, Special Programs	$37,840	$32,000	$44,678	51
98.0	Dean, Undergraduate Programs	$46,300	$40,483	$49,349	9

Reprinted by permission from *1986–87 Administrative Compensation Survey,* Copyright 1987 by College and University Personnel Association, 1986–87, table 19, p. 19.

A-15 Weighted Average Salary and Average Compensation, by Category, Affiliation, and Academic Rank, 1986–87[1]

Academic Rank	All Combined	Public	Private Independent	Church-Related
	SALARY			
Doctoral-level institutions				
Professor	50,500	48,740	56,900	51,120
Associate Prof.	36,210	35,590	38,820	37,440
Assistant Prof.	30,360	29,930	32,040	30,490
Instructor	22,130	21,440	24,890	26,260
Lecturer	26,090	26,060	26,650	24,310
All Ranks	39,800	38,670	44,620	39,030
Comprehensive institutions				
Professor	42,160	42,290	42,680	39,800
Associate Prof.	33,200	33,340	33,140	32,130
Assistant Prof.	27,310	27,520	26,650	26,670
Instructor	21,220	21,640	19,070	21,180
Lecturer	22,790	22,470	24,210	26,530
All Ranks	33,750	34,050	33,010	32,140
General baccalaureate institutions				
Professor	36,170	36,870	40,460	32,480
Associate Prof.	29,210	31,210	30,650	26,910
Assistant Prof.	24,070	25,940	24,990	22,500
Instructor	19,840	21,590	19,520	18,990
Lecturer	23,240	22,810	26,250	19,130
All Ranks	28,480	29,660	30,780	26,170
Two-year institutions with academic ranks				
Professor	37,170	37,460	27,210	23,890
Associate Prof.	31,330	31,560	24,720	21,330
Assistant Prof.	26,590	26,940	20,030	19,200
Instructor	22,270	22,750	16,190	16,570
Lecturer	19,540	19,540	—	—
All Ranks	30,100	30,490	21,120	20,310
Two-year institutions without academic ranks				
No Rank	31,240	31,430	20,280	19,830
All catagories except two-year institutions without academic ranks				
Professor	45,530	45,280	50,270	37,620
Associate Prof.	33,820	34,170	34,910	30,090
Assistant Prof.	27,920	28,470	28,310	24,600
Instructor	21,330	31,810	20,440	19,900
Lecturer	24,930	24,730	26,410	24,080
All Ranks	35,470	35,790	37,760	29,670

1 Sample includes 1,875 institutions.

Reprinted by permission from *Academe*, March–April 1987, table 3, copyright by The American Association of University Professors.

All Combined	Public	Private Independent	Church-Related
		COMPENSATION	
61,130	58,720	69,780	62,440
44,350	43,410	48,250	46,200
37,070	36,580	39,080	36,790
27,130	26,340	30,450	31,260
32,110	32,180	32,470	29,190
48,430	46,910	54,830	47,660
51,190	51,200	52,600	48,540
40,670	40,780	40,890	39,380
33,340	33,670	32,340	32,250
25,820	26,410	22,840	25,650
28,110	27,750	29,300	32,460
41,130	41,450	40,500	39,150
44,440	44,770	50,170	39,780
35,620	38,160	37,690	32,800
29,050	31,610	30,260	26,930
23,620	26,240	23,050	22,400
28,190	27,690	32,290	22,240
34,710	36,120	37,760	31,710
46,340	46,730	33,120	29,290
39,010	39,340	29,660	25,860
33,310	33,800	24,110	23,220
28,000	28,690	19,360	19,740
25,120	25,120	—	—
37,600	38,130	25,420	24,610
37,550	37,790	23,900	23,760
55,300	54,770	61,820	45,990
41,460	41,810	43,180	36,830
34,090	34,900	34,420	29,560
26,040	26,860	24,510	23,610
30,690	20,550	32,190	28,970
43,250	43,580	46,350	36,060

Percentiles of the Distributions of Institutions by Average Salary and Average Compensation, 1986–87 (Rounded to Nearest $100)

Rating[1]	1*	1	2	3	4	1*	1	2	3	4
Percentile	95	80	60	40	20	95	80	60	40	20
	SALARY					COMPENSATION				
Doctoral-level institutions										
Professor	62,4	55,9	50,3	46,7	42,8	77,3	68,4	61,7	56,3	51,3
Associate	42,8	39,4	37,0	35,3	32,5	53,4	48,3	45,5	43,0	39,3
Assistant	35,7	32,9	30,6	29,3	27,8	43,6	40,0	37,4	35,6	33,6
Instructor	29,3	25,8	23,8	22,4	20,5	35,3	31,6	29,4	27,6	24,8
Comprehensive institutions										
Professor	49,1	44,3	40,4	37,8	34,6	60,1	55,0	49,7	45,7	41,3
Associate	38,2	35,6	33,0	31,3	28,8	47,4	44,6	40,7	38,1	34,6
Assistant	31,3	29,5	27,5	26,1	24,7	39,1	36,4	34,0	31,6	29,5
Instructor	27,2	24,6	22,5	21,2	19,7	34,0	30,1	27,6	25,7	23,7
General baccalaureate institutions										
Professor	46,2	38,5	34,2	30,5	27,1	56,9	47,8	41,3	36,5	32,5
Associate	35,2	31,5	28,6	26,1	23,3	43,7	38,6	34,6	31,5	27,6
Assistant	28,4	25,9	24,1	22,4	20,3	34,7	31,4	29,0	26,8	24,0
Instructor	25,5	22,4	20,5	18,9	17,5	30,8	27,1	24,4	22,5	20,5
Two-year institutions with academic ranks										
Professor	41,8	38,5	35,3	32,5	30,1	51,0	47,7	44,3	40,3	36,4
Associate	36,0	32,8	30,6	28,7	25,8	44,9	41,0	38,2	35,2	31,4
Assistant	30,5	27,9	26,2	24,4	21,5	39,6	34,6	32,5	30,4	26,6
Instructor	27,4	23,8	22,3	20,8	18,7	34,2	30,0	28,4	26,4	22,9
Two-year institutions without academic ranks										
No Rank	40,5	35,0	29,5	26,3	22,5	48,6	43,4	36,1	34,8	27,1

1 Interpretation of the ratings: 1* = 95th percentile; 1 = 80th percentile; 2 = 60 percentile; etc. Average Salary and/or Compensation lower than the 10th percentile will be rated 5. An average salary of 52,0 for the rank of professor in doctoral-level institutions would be rated 2 because it falls between the 60th and 80th percentiles or is higher than 50,3 but less than 55,9, which is the average salary needed for a rating of 1 or the salary level of the 80th percentile.

Reprinted by permission from *Academe*, March–April 1987, table 6, copyright by The American Association of University Professors.

Year	Full-Time Faculty	Part-Time Faculty	Total Faculty	Professional Staff	Administrative Staff
1986[1]	110,909	164,080	274,989	26,397	21,370
1985[1]	110,179	162,533	272,712	26,046	21,019
1984	109,064	143,205	252,269	17,396	19,141
1983	109,436	142,170	251,606	17,147	18,228
1982	99,701	137,060	236,761	16,185	18,634
1981	104,558	139,670	244,228	14,927	17,938
1980	104,777	134,064	238,841	16,389	17,835
1979	92,881	119,993	212,874	16,155	16,609
1978	95,461	118,251	213,712	15,077	16,705
1977	89,089	116,439	205,528	12,722	15,633
1976	88,277	111,378	199,691	13,180	15,653

1 Beginning in 1985, staffing data is weighted by enrollment to adjust unreported staff totals. Prior to 1985, faculty data was usually compiled for all colleges, while professional and administrative staff was underreported.

Source: AACJC Annual Survey of Colleges, 1976–1986.

Race, Age, and Date	Percentage, by Years of School Completed			
	Less Than 5 Years of Elementary School	4 Years of High School or More	4 or More Years of College	Median School Years Completed
ALL RACES				
25 and over				
1010[1]	23.8	13.5	2.7	8.1
1920[1]	22.0	16.4	3.3	8.2
1930[1]	17.5	19.1	3.9	8.4
April 1940	13.7	24.5	4.6	8.6
April 1950	11.1	34.3	6.2	9.3
April 1960	8.3	41.1	7.7	10.5
March 1970	5.3	55.2	11.0	12.2
March 1975	4.2	62.5	13.9	12.3
March 1980	3.4	68.6	17.0	12.5
March 1982	3.0	71.0	17.7	12.6
March 1985	2.7	73.9	19.4	12.6
25–29				
April 1940	5.9	38.1	5.9	10.3
April 1950	4.6	52.8	7.7	12.1
April 1960	2.8	60.7	11.0	12.3
March 1970	1.1	75.4	16.4	12.6
March 1975	1.0	83.1	21.9	12.8
March 1980	0.8	85.4	22.5	12.9
March 1982	0.8	86.2	21.7	12.8
March 1985	0.7	86.1	22.2	12.9
WHITE[2]				
25 and over				
April 1940	10.9	26.1	4.9	8.7
April 1950	8.9	36.4	6.6	9.7
April 1960	6.7	43.2	8.1	10.8
March 1970	4.2	57.4	11.6	12.2
March 1975	3.3	64.5	14.5	12.4
March 1980	2.6	70.5	17.8	12.5
March 1982	2.4	72.8	18.5	12.6
March 1985	2.2	75.5	20.0	12.7

NOTE: Data for 1975 and subsequent years are for the noninstitutional population. Some data have been revised from previously published figures.

1 Estimates based on retrojection, by the Bureau of the Census, of 1940 census data on education by age.

2 Persons of Hispanic origin are included, as appropriate, in the "white" or in the "black and other races" category.

Race, Age, and Date	Percentage, by Years of School Completed			Median School Years Completed
	Less Than 5 Years of Elementary School	4 Years of High School or More	4 or More Years of College	
WHITE (Continued)				
25–29				
1920[1]	12.9	22.0	4.5	8.5
April 1940	3.4	41.2	6.4	10.7
April 1950	3.3	56.3	8.2	12.2
April 1960	2.2	63.7	11.8	12.3
March 1970	0.9	77.8	17.3	12.6
March 1975	1.0	84.4	22.8	12.8
March 1980	0.8	86.9	23.7	12.9
March 1982	0.8	86.9	22.7	12.9
March 1985	0.8	86.8	23.2	12.9
BLACK AND OTHER RACES[2]				
25 and over				
April 1940	41.8	7.7	1.3	5.7
April 1950	32.6	13.7	2.2	6.9
April 1960	23.5	21.7	3.5	8.2
March 1970	14.7	36.1	6.1	10.1
March 1975	11.7	46.4	9.2	11.4
March 1980	8.8	54.6	11.1	12.2
March 1982	7.4	58.1	12.4	12.3
March 1985	6.0	63.2	15.4	12.4
25–29				
1920[1]	44.6	6.3	1.2	5.4
April 1940	27.0	12.3	1.6	7.1
April 1950	16.1	23.6	2.8	8.7
April 1960	7.2	38.6	5.4	10.8
March 1970	2.2	58.4	10.0	12.2
March 1975	0.7	73.8	15.4	12.6
March 1980	1.0	77.0	15.2	12.7
March 1982	0.7	82.2	15.8	12.8
March 1985	0.5	82.4	16.7	12.8

Source: *Digest of Education Statistics, 1987*, table 8, p. 13.

A-19 Years of School Completed, by Race, Sex, and Age: 1985 (Persons 25 Years Old and Over, as of March 1985)

Race, Sex, and Age	Population (1,000)	Elementary School 0–4 Years	5–7 Years	8 Years	High School 1–3 Years	4 Years	College 1–3 Years	4 Years or More	Median School Years Completed
All races	143,524	2.7	4.8	6.4	12.2	38.2	16.3	19.4	12.6
Male	67,756	2.9	5.0	6.3	11.5	34.8	16.5	23.1	12.7
Female	75,768	2.5	4.5	6.5	12.9	41.3	16.2	16.0	12.6
25–29 years	21,106	.7	1.5	1.7	10.0	42.4	21.6	22.2	12.9
30–34 years	19,752	1.0	1.5	1.8	8.1	39.5	22.4	25.6	12.9
35–44 years	31,299	1.3	2.3	2.7	9.8	38.6	19.2	26.2	12.9
45–54 years	22,398	2.2	4.3	5.0	13.0	42.4	14.4	18.6	12.6
55 years old and over	48,969	5.3	9.2	13.3	16.1	33.7	10.6	11.7	12.2
Black	14,820	6.2	8.6	6.2	19.2	33.9	14.8	11.1	12.3
25–29 years	2,617	.4	1.0	2.1	16.0	46.2	22.9	11.5	12.7
30–34 years	2,289	1.2	1.9	2.7	15.6	42.2	20.1	16.3	12.7
35–44 years	3,270	1.9	3.6	3.2	19.7	38.1	18.3	15.2	12.6
45–54 years	2,359	3.9	8.8	7.5	23.4	33.9	12.8	9.7	12.2
55 years old and over	4,285	16.9	20.6	12.1	20.6	18.8	5.3	5.5	9.0
Spanish origin[1]	8,455	13.5	15.5	8.7	14.3	28.4	11.0	8.5	11.5
25–29 years	1,693	6.0	11.4	5.4	16.3	34.0	15.9	11.0	12.3
30–34 years	1,397	7.9	12.5	6.9	16.9	31.5	14.3	9.7	12.2
35–44 years	2,139	11.0	14.4	8.2	14.6	29.4	13.2	9.3	12.1
45–54 years	1,366	13.1	18.5	9.0	14.0	30.2	8.0	7.4	10.8
55 years old and over	1,860	27.6	20.5	13.6	10.5	18.7	3.9	5.1	8.1

Percentage of Population Completing—

1 Persons of Spanish origin may be of any race.

Source: *Statistical Abstract, 1987*, table 199, p. 122.

A-20 Years of School Completed by Persons[1] Age 18 and Over, by Age, Sex, and Race/Ethnicity: United States, 1985 (in Thousands)

Age, Sex, and Race	Total Population[1]	Elementary Level		High School		College		
		Less Than 8 Years	8 Years	1–3 Years	4 Years	1–3 Years	4 Years	5 Years or More
Total								
18 and over	171,368	11,241	9,748	22,621	67,086	30,913	17,748	12,014
18–19 years old	7,379	128	157	2,520	3,590	979	3	—
20–24 years old	20,465	415	397	2,548	8,630	6,528	1,669	283
25 years old and over	143,524	10,699	9,193	17,553	54,866	23,406	16,077	11,731
25–29 years old	21,106	465	350	2,109	8,951	4,551	3,270	1,411
30–34 years old	19,751	510	364	1,594	7,797	4,430	3,095	1,961
35–39 years old	17,222	491	405	1,490	6,519	3,420	2,553	2,345
40–49 years old	25,586	1,309	986	2,955	10,522	4,316	2,770	2,728
50–59 years old	22,320	1,830	1,499	3,352	9,077	2,864	2,010	1,689
60–69 years old	19,980	2,414	2,185	3,227	7,596	2,164	1,366	1,028
70 years old and over	17,557	3,676	3,403	2,827	4,402	1,663	1,016	569
Men								
18 and over	81,451	5,668	4,535	10,456	29,437	14,752	9,269	7,335
18–19 years old	3,640	86	85	1,362	1,678	428	2	—
20–24 years old	10,055	246	212	1,311	4,207	3,160	768	152
25 years old and over	67,756	5,336	4,238	7,785	23,552	11,164	8,499	7,183
25–29 years old	10,420	258	163	1,053	4,339	2,201	1,602	804
30–34 years old	9,764	260	213	771	3,616	2,233	1,548	1,126
35–39 years old	8,460	265	185	686	2,800	1,714	1,440	1,371
40–49 years old	12,472	714	520	1,374	4,476	2,083	1,535	1,768
50–59 years old	10,707	1,001	789	1,504	3,753	1,351	1,162	1,148
60–69 years old	9,066	1,205	1,057	1,352	3,034	984	775	660
70 years old and over	6,867	1,633	1,311	1,045	1,534	601	438	306

(Continued)

Age, Sex, and Race	Total Population[1]	Elementary Level		High School		College		
		Less Than 8 Years	8 Years	1–3 Years	4 Years	1–3 Years	4 Years	5 Years or More
Women								
18 and over	89,917	5,570	5,212	12,166	37,647	16,162	8,480	4,679
18–19 years old	3,738	43	72	1,160	1,911	552	1	—
20–24 years old	10,411	167	185	1,237	4,422	3,369	901	131
25 years old and over	75,768	5,360	4,955	9,769	31,314	12,241	7,578	4,548
25–29 years old	10,686	207	187	1,056	4,612	2,350	1,668	607
30–34 years old	9,987	250	151	823	4,182	2,197	1,547	835
35–39 years old	8,762	226	220	804	3,719	1,706	1,113	974
40–49 years old	13,114	595	466	1,581	6,046	2,231	1,235	960
50–59 years old	11,613	829	710	1,848	5,324	1,515	848	541
60–69 years old	10,914	1,209	1,128	1,875	4,562	1,180	591	368
70 years old and over	10,690	2,043	2,092	1,782	2,868	1,062	578	263
White[2]								
18 and over	148,128	8,588	8,547	18,318	58,958	27,032	15,816	10,868
18–19 years old	6,051	105	108	1,949	3,039	849	2	—
20–24 years old	17,172	360	337	2,004	7,191	5,532	1,505	242
25 years old and over	124,905	8,123	8,101	14,365	48,728	20,651	14,309	10,626
25–29 years old	17,829	417	286	1,644	7,537	3,811	2,877	1,257
30–34 years old	16,846	403	293	1,192	6,660	3,842	2,706	1,751
35–39 years old	14,844	410	345	1,135	5,638	2,959	2,248	2,110
40–49 years old	22,062	1,018	785	2,289	9,331	3,798	2,404	2,435
50–59 years old	19,570	1,333	1,250	2,720	8,232	2,616	1,856	1,563
60–69 years old	17,833	1,743	1,944	2,785	7,092	2,042	1,262	965
70 years old and over	15,922	2,802	3,198	2,600	4,237	1,582	957	545
Black[2]								
18 and over	18,606	2,251	1,013	3,786	6,725	3,071	1,121	641
18–19 years old	1,092	22	42	472	457	99	—	—
20–24 years old	2,694	34	53	462	1,241	783	97	24
25 years old and over	14,820	2,195	918	2,852	5,027	2,189	1,024	616
25–29 years old	2,617	35	54	419	1,210	598	231	71
30–34 years old	2,289	72	62	357	966	462	247	125
35–39 years old	1,803	63	42	304	721	375	172	125

40–49 years old	2,687	232	157	597	962	401	185	152
50–59 years old	2,226	407	221	572	665	198	85	81
60–69 years old	1,769	591	210	392	368	97	68	43
70 years old and over	1,428	794	172	211	135	58	38	20
Hispanic origin[3]								
18 and over	10,849	2,778	869	1,851	3,215	1,349	465	320
18–19 years old	626	64	30	279	214	39	—	—
20–24 years old	1,768	261	101	362	599	377	57	11
25 years old and over	8,455	2,454	738	1,210	2,402	932	408	309
25–29 years old	1,693	294	91	276	576	269	129	58
30–34 years old	1,397	287	97	236	440	200	77	59
35–39 years old	1,150	264	90	171	336	169	59	61
40–49 years old	1,751	514	155	252	523	180	75	51
50–59 years old	1,197	427	123	159	329	75	42	45
60–69 years old	759	352	115	79	137	33	16	24
70 years old and over	508	314	67	36	61	8	11	10

NOTE: Data are based on sample surveys of the civilian noninstitutional population.

1   Civilian noninstitutional population.

2   Includes persons of Hispanic origin.

3   Persons of Hispanic origin may be of any race.

—   Data not available.

Source: *Digest of Education Statistics, 1987*, table 9, pp. 14–15.

Region, Division, and State	Population, 25 Years Old and Over (1,000)	Percentage of Population Completing at Least—			
		High School		College	
		1–3 Years	4 Years	1–3 Years	4 or More Years
United States	132,836	81.7	66.5	31.9	16.2
Northeast	29,903	82.4	67.1	30.8	17.2
New England	7,438	84.3	70.5	34.6	19.2
Maine	662	83.4	68.7	29.4	14.4
New Hampshire	542	85.3	72.3	35.1	18.2
Vermont	295	83.3	71.0	34.7	19.0
Massachusetts	3,463	85.6	72.2	35.8	20.0
Rhode Island	575	79.3	61.1	28.3	15.4
Connecticut	1,900	83.7	70.3	35.9	20.7
Middle Atlantic	22,466	81.8	66.0	29.5	16.6
New York	10,721	81.7	66.3	32.2	17.9
New Jersey	4,504	82.3	67.4	31.5	18.3
Pennsylvania	7,240	81.6	64.7	24.3	13.6
Midwest	34,085	82.9	68.0	29.4	14.7
East North Central	24,066	83.4	67.3	28.7	14.5
Ohio	6,292	84.6	67.0	26.5	13.7
Indiana	3,136	83.4	66.4	24.6	12.5
Illinois	6,679	81.5	66.5	31.4	16.2
Michigan	5,254	84.9	68.0	30.0	14.3
Wisconsin	2,705	82.0	69.6	29.2	14.8
West North Central	10,019	81.8	69.6	31.1	15.3
Minnesota	2,346	83.3	73.1	34.5	17.4
Iowa	1,700	83.3	71.5	28.6	13.9
Missouri	2,919	78.3	63.5	27.2	13.9
North Dakota	365	75.2	66.4	35.1	14.8
South Dakota	390	78.0	67.9	31.7	14.0
Nebraska	912	84.9	73.4	32.8	15.5
Kansas	1,388	85.4	73.3	34.2	17.0
South	43,691	77.4	60.2	29.4	15.0
South Atlantic	21,994	78.9	61.3	30.3	15.7
Delaware	345	85.2	68.6	32.4	17.5
Maryland	2,499	83.5	67.4	34.9	20.4

Region, Division, and State	Population, 25 Years Old and Over (1,000)	Percentage of Population Completing at Least—			
		High School		College	
		1–3 Years	4 Years	1–3 Years	4 or More Years
District of Columbia	399	83.0	67.1	41.5	27.5
Virginia	3,133	78.4	62.4	34.0	19.1
West Virginia	1,147	72.0	56.0	20.4	10.4
North Carolina	3,403	75.4	54.8	27.0	13.2
South Carolina	1,733	74.3	53.7	26.7	13.4
Georgia	3,086	76.3	56.4	27.9	14.6
Florida	6,250	82.4	66.7	31.6	14.9
East South Central	8,364	72.2	55.3	24.1	12.1
Kentucky	2,087	68.7	53.1	21.8	11.1
Tennessee	2,692	72.3	56.2	24.5	12.6
Alabama	2,217	75.0	56.5	24.7	12.2
Mississippi	1,368	73.0	54.8	25.6	12.3
West South Central	13,333	78.3	61.5	31.1	15.5
Arkansas	1,337	73.2	55.5	22.3	10.8
Louisiana	2,281	75.1	57.7	26.7	13.9
Oklahoma	1,770	81.6	66.0	31.2	15.1
Texas	7,944	79.3	62.6	33.8	16.9
West	25,157	86.8	74.5	40.9	19.3
Mountain	6,335	87.6	75.2	39.5	18.8
Montana	451	85.7	74.4	36.5	17.5
Idaho	514	87.4	73.7	37.2	15.8
Wyoming	255	90.0	77.9	37.9	17.2
Colorado	1,664	89.4	78.6	44.1	23.0
New Mexico	707	82.3	68.9	34.7	17.6
Arizona	1,559	85.0	72.4	38.0	17.4
Utah	705	93.0	80.0	44.1	19.9
Nevada	480	90.4	75.5	35.1	14.4
Pacific	18,822	86.5	74.3	41.4	19.4
Washington	2,439	89.7	77.6	40.2	19.0
Oregon	1,580	88.5	75.6	38.5	17.9
California	14,044	85.8	73.5	42.0	19.6
Alaska	211	91.0	82.5	43.7	21.1
Hawaii	548	83.8	73.8	38.8	20.3

Source: *Statistical Abstract, 1986,* table 217, p. 134.

Percentage of Population* with Less Than 5 Years of School and with 4 Years of High School or More, by Age, Race, and Spanish Origin: 1970–1985

Race and Spanish Origin	Less Than 5 Years of School			1985				
	1970	1975	1980	Total	25–34	35–44	45–64	65 and over
All races[1]	5.5	4.2	3.6	2.7	.9	1.3	2.9	6.7
White	4.5	3.3	2.6	2.2	.8	1.2	2.3	5.0
Black	14.6	12.3	8.2	6.2	.8	1.9	6.7	23.3
Spanish origin[2]	19.5	18.5	15.5	13.5	6.9	11.0	17.1	34.6
Mexican	28.5	24.6	20.1	17.1	8.9	14.0	22.5	47.2
Puerto Rican	20.5	17.4	14.1	12.8	4.1	10.5	20.0	(B)
Cuban	8.2	7.3	7.3	7.4	.6	3.8	7.4	16.9
Other[3]	8.8	7.6	8.3	6.7	3.9	5.7	7.5	16.9

Race and Spanish Origin	4 Years of High School or More			1985				
	1970	1975	1980	Total	25–34	35–44	45–64	65 and over
All races[1]	52.3	62.5	66.5	73.9	86.8	84.0	70.5	48.2
White	54.5	64.6	68.8	75.5	87.8	85.4	73.2	50.6
Black	31.4	42.5	51.2	59.8	79.7	71.6	47.9	22.0
Spanish origin[2]	32.1	37.9	44.0	47.9	58.5	51.8	40.0	21.1
Mexican	24.2	31.0	37.6	41.9	51.9	47.8	31.3	11.2
Puerto Rican	23.4	28.7	40.1	46.3	62.7	45.3	33.5	(B)
Cuban	43.9	51.7	55.3	51.1	75.3	56.0	47.1	30.2
Other[3]	44.9	58.0	57.4	64.2	72.6	65.6	62.0	39.0

* Persons 25 years old and over, as of April 1970 and 1980, and March 1975 and 1985.

1 Includes races not shown separately.

2 Persons of Spanish origin may be of any race.

3 Includes Central or South American and other Spanish origin.

(B). Base too small to meet standards of reliability.

Source: *Statistical Abstract, 1987*, table 200, p. 122.

A-23 Enrollment Status for Persons* 3–34 Years Old by Age, Sex, Race, Spanish Origin, and Mexican Origin: October 1983

Age, Sex, Race, Spanish Origin, and Mexican Origin	Population	Enrolled in School — Total		Below College Level¹		In College		Not Enrolled in School — Total		High-School Graduate		Not High-School Graduate	
		Number	Percentage	Number	Percentage	Number	Percentage	Number	Percentage	Number	Percentage	Number	Percentage
ALL RACES													
Total, 3–34 years	119,415	57,744	48.4	46,920	39.3	10,825	9.1	61,670	51.6	46,647	39.1	15,024	12.6
3–4 years	6,988	2,624	37.5	2,624	37.5	—	—	4,364	62.5	—	—	4,364	62.5
5–6 years	6,510	6,214	95.4	6,214	95.4	—	—	296	4.6	—	—	296	4.6
7–9 years	9,512	9,408	98.9	9,408	98.9	—	—	104	1.1	—	—	104	1.1
10–13 years	13,951	13,870	99.4	13,870	99.4	—	—	81	0.6	—	—	81	0.6
14–15 years	7,214	7,093	98.3	7,085	98.2	8	0.1	121	1.7	—	—	121	1.7
16–17 years	7,304	6,698	91.7	6,446	88.3	252	3.5	606	8.3	111	1.5	494	6.8
18–19 years	7,819	3,938	50.4	998	12.8	2,940	37.6	3,881	49.6	2,748	35.1	1,132	14.5
20–21 years	8,039	2,609	32.5	114	1.4	2,495	31.0	5,430	67.5	4,143	51.5	1,287	16.0
22–24 years	12,722	2,111	16.6	69	0.5	2,042	16.1	10,611	83.4	8,620	67.8	1,991	15.7
25–29 years	20,606	1,976	9.6	55	0.3	1,921	9.3	18,630	90.4	15,841	76.9	2,789	13.5
30–34 years	18,750	1,203	6.4	37	0.2	1,167	6.2	17,547	93.6	15,183	81.0	2,364	12.6
Male, 3–34 years	59,534	29,593	49.7	24,089	40.5	5,504	9.2	29,941	50.3	22,287	37.4	7,654	12.9
3–4 years	3,573	1,363	38.1	1,363	38.1	—	—	2,211	61.9	—	—	2,211	61.9
5–6 years	3,329	3,166	95.1	3,166	95.1	—	—	163	4.9	—	—	163	4.9
7–9 years	4,864	4,805	98.8	4,805	98.8	—	—	59	1.2	—	—	59	1.2
10–13 years	7,130	7,082	99.3	7,082	99.3	—	—	48	0.7	—	—	48	0.7
14–15 years	3,676	3,617	98.4	3,615	98.3	2	—	59	1.6	—	—	59	1.6
16–17 years	3,709	3,404	91.8	3,298	88.9	107	2.9	305	8.2	53	1.4	252	6.8
18–19 years	3,877	1,956	50.4	616	15.9	1,340	34.6	1,921	49.6	1,291	33.3	630	16.3
20–21 years	3,919	1,379	35.2	69	1.8	1,310	33.4	2,540	64.8	1,872	47.8	668	17.0
22–24 years	6,207	1,203	19.4	33	0.5	1,170	18.9	5,004	80.6	3,923	63.2	1,081	17.4
25–29 years	10,092	1,084	10.7	29	0.3	1,055	10.5	9,008	89.3	7,673	76.0	1,334	13.2
30–34 years	9,157	534	5.8	13	0.1	521	5.7	8,623	94.2	7,474	81.6	1,149	12.5
Female, 3–34 years	59,881	28,152	47.0	22,831	38.1	5,321	8.9	31,729	53.0	24,360	40.7	7,369	12.3
3–4 years	3,415	1,261	36.9	1,261	36.9	—	—	2,154	63.1	—	—	2,154	63.1
5–6 years	3,181	3,048	95.8	3,048	95.8	—	—	133	4.2	—	—	133	4.2
7–9 years	4,647	4,603	99.0	4,603	99.0	—	—	45	1.0	—	—	45	1.0
10–13 years	6,821	6,788	99.5	6,788	99.5	—	—	33	0.5	—	—	33	0.5
14–15 years	3,538	3,476	98.2	3,470	98.1	6	0.2	62	1.8	—	—	62	1.8

(Continued)

Appendix Table A-23, Continued

Age, Sex, Race, Spanish Origin, and Mexican Origin	Population	Enrolled in School						Not Enrolled in School					
		Total		Below College Level[1]		In College		Total		High-School Graduate		Not High-School Graduate	
	Number	Number	Percentage	Number	Percentage	Number	Percentage	Number	Percentage	Number	Percentage	Number	Percentage
16–17 years	3,595	3,294	91.6	3,148	87.6	147	4.1	301	8.4	59	1.6	242	6.7
18–19 years	3,942	1,983	50.3	383	9.7	1,600	40.6	1,959	49.7	1,457	37.0	502	12.7
20–21 years	4,120	1,230	29.9	45	1.1	1,185	28.8	2,890	70.1	2,271	55.1	619	15.0
22–24 years	6,515	908	13.9	36	0.5	872	13.4	5,607	86.1	4,697	72.1	910	14.0
25–29 years	10,514	892	8.5	26	0.3	865	8.2	9,622	91.5	8,168	77.7	1,454	13.8
30–34 years	9,593	669	7.0	24	0.3	645	6.7	8,924	93.0	7,709	80.4	1,215	12.7
WHITE													
Total, 3–34 years	99,325	47,423	47.7	38,181	38.4	9,242	9.3	51,902	52.3	39,954	40.2	11,949	12.0
3–4 years	5,668	2,132	37.6	2,132	37.6	—	—	3,536	62.4	—	—	3,536	62.4
5–6 years	5,321	5,094	95.7	5,094	95.7	—	—	226	4.3	—	—	226	4.3
7–9 years	7,730	7,642	98.9	7,642	98.9	—	—	88	1.1	—	—	88	1.1
10–13 years	11,366	11,292	99.3	11,292	99.3	—	—	74	0.7	—	—	74	0.7
14–15 years	5,955	5,857	98.4	5,852	98.3	6	0.1	98	1.6	—	—	98	1.6
16–17 years	6,007	5,492	91.4	5,284	88.0	208	3.5	515	8.6	91	1.5	424	7.1
18–19 years	6,452	3,285	50.9	688	10.7	2,597	40.3	3,167	49.1	2,283	35.4	884	13.7
20–21 years	6,738	2,253	33.4	91	1.4	2,161	32.1	4,485	66.6	3,472	51.5	1,013	15.0
22–24 years	10,709	1,753	16.4	48	0.4	1,705	15.9	8,956	83.6	7,425	69.3	1,531	14.3
25–29 years	17,430	1,641	9.4	38	0.2	1,603	9.2	15,789	90.6	13,545	77.7	2,244	12.9
30–34 years	15,949	981	6.2	20	0.1	961	6.0	14,968	93.8	13,138	82.4	1,830	11.5
Male, 3–34 years	49,855	24,368	48.9	19,650	39.4	4,718	9.5	25,487	51.1	19,305	38.7	6,181	12.4
3–4 years	2,916	1,115	38.2	1,115	38.2	—	—	1,801	61.8	—	—	1,801	61.8
5–6 years	2,744	2,609	95.1	2,609	95.1	—	—	135	4.9	—	—	135	4.9
7–9 years	3,953	3,904	98.8	3,904	98.8	—	—	48	1.2	—	—	48	1.2
10–13 years	5,820	5,778	99.3	5,778	99.3	—	—	42	0.7	—	—	42	0.7
14–15 years	3,051	3,000	98.3	2,999	98.3	2	0.1	51	1.7	—	—	51	1.7
16–17 years	3,046	2,791	91.6	2,706	88.8	85	2.8	255	8.4	36	1.2	219	7.2
18–19 years	3,216	1,630	50.7	433	13.5	1,197	37.2	1,586	49.3	1,085	33.7	500	15.6
20–21 years	3,285	1,201	36.6	52	1.6	1,149	35.0	2,084	63.4	1,561	47.5	523	15.9
22–24 years	5,286	1,014	19.2	25	0.5	989	18.7	4,272	80.8	3,430	64.9	842	15.9
25–29 years	8,656	899	10.4	23	0.3	875	10.1	7,757	89.6	6,635	76.7	1,122	13.0
30–34 years	7,883	427	5.4	6	0.1	421	5.3	7,456	94.6	6,558	83.2	898	11.4
Female, 3–34 years	49,470	23,054	46.6	18,530	37.5	4,524	9.1	26,416	53.4	20,648	41.7	5,767	11.7
3–4 years	2,752	1,017	36.9	1,017	36.9	—	—	1,736	63.1	—	—	1,736	63.1
5–6 years	2,577	2,486	96.5	2,486	96.5	—	—	91	3.5	—	—	91	3.5
7–9 years	3,777	3,738	99.0	3,738	99.0	—	—	39	1.0	—	—	39	1.0
10–13 years	5,547	5,514	99.4	5,514	99.4	—	—	32	0.6	—	—	32	0.6
14–15 years	2,904	2,857	98.4	2,853	98.2	4	0.1	47	1.6	—	—	47	1.6

16–17 years	2,961	2,701	91.2	2,576	87.1	123	4.1	260	8.8	55	1.9	205	6.9
18–19 years	3,236	1,655	51.1	255	7.9	1,400	43.3	1,581	48.9	1,198	37.0	383	11.8
20–21 years	3,453	1,051	30.5	39	1.1	1,012	29.3	2,402	69.5	1,911	55.3	491	14.2
22–24 years	5,423	739	13.6	23	0.4	717	13.2	4,684	86.4	3,995	73.7	689	12.7
25–29 years	8,774	742	8.5	14	0.2	728	8.3	8,032	91.5	6,910	78.8	1,122	12.8
30–34 years	8,066	554	6.9	14	0.2	540	6.7	7,512	93.1	6,580	81.6	932	11.6
BLACK												
Total, 3–34 years	16,156	8,200	50.8	7,097	43.9	1,102	6.8	7,957	49.2	5,397	33.4	2,560	15.8
3–4 years	1,070	387	36.2	387	36.2	—	—	683	63.8	—	—	683	63.8
5–6 years	967	915	94.7	915	94.7	—	—	51	5.3	—	—	51	5.3
7–9 years	1,417	1,405	99.1	1,405	99.1	—	—	13	0.9	—	—	13	0.9
10–13 years	2,071	2,065	99.7	2,065	99.7	—	—	6	0.3	—	—	6	0.3
14–15 years	1,058	1,035	97.8	1,035	97.8	—	—	24	2.2	—	—	24	2.2
16–17 years	1,082	1,002	92.6	971	89.7	31	2.9	80	7.4	18	1.6	62	5.8
18–19 years	1,134	523	46.1	265	23.4	258	22.7	611	53.9	412	36.4	199	17.5
20–21 years	1,102	258	23.4	16	1.4	242	22.0	844	76.6	608	55.1	237	21.5
22–24 years	1,629	254	15.6	12	0.8	241	14.8	1,376	84.4	979	60.1	396	24.3
25–29 years	2,480	193	7.8	14	0.6	179	7.2	2,287	92.2	1,824	73.5	463	18.7
30–34 years	2,145	164	7.6	13	0.6	151	7.0	1,981	92.4	1,556	72.5	425	19.8
Male, 3–34 years	7,730	4,088	52.9	3,591	46.5	497	6.4	3,642	47.1	2,389	30.9	1,252	16.2
3–4 years	539	200	37.1	200	37.1	—	—	339	62.9	—	—	339	62.9
5–6 years	487	467	95.8	467	95.8	—	—	21	4.2	—	—	21	4.2
7–9 years	715	707	98.9	707	98.9	—	—	8	1.1	—	—	8	1.1
10–13 years	1,042	1,036	99.4	1,036	99.4	—	—	6	0.6	—	—	6	0.6
14–15 years	531	522	98.4	522	98.4	—	—	8	1.6	—	—	8	1.6
16–17 years	534	491	91.8	479	89.6	12	2.2	44	8.2	14	2.7	29	5.5
18–19 years	539	251	46.6	158	29.3	93	17.3	288	53.4	182	33.8	106	19.6
20–21 years	520	122	23.5	11	2.1	112	21.5	398	76.5	275	52.9	123	23.6
22–24 years	748	129	17.2	3	0.4	126	16.8	620	82.8	414	55.3	206	27.5
25–29 years	1,115	95	8.5	4	0.4	91	8.2	1,020	91.5	828	74.3	192	17.2
30–34 years	960	69	7.1	5	0.5	64	6.7	891	92.9	676	70.4	215	22.4
Female, 3–34 years	8,427	4,112	48.8	3,507	41.6	605	7.2	4,315	51.2	3,007	35.7	1,307	15.5
3–4 years	532	187	35.2	187	35.2	—	—	344	64.8	—	—	344	64.8
5–6 years	479	449	93.6	449	93.6	—	—	31	6.4	—	—	31	6.4
7–9 years	703	698	99.3	698	99.3	—	—	5	0.7	—	—	5	0.7
10–13 years	1,029	1,029	100.0	1,029	100.0	—	—	—	—	—	—	—	—
14–15 years	527	512	97.1	512	97.1	—	—	15	2.9	—	—	15	2.9
16–17 years	548	511	93.4	492	89.9	19	3.5	36	6.6	3	0.6	33	6.0
18–19 years	595	272	45.7	107	18.0	164	27.6	323	54.3	230	38.7	93	15.6
20–21 years	582	136	23.3	5	0.9	131	22.4	447	76.7	333	57.1	114	19.6
22–24 years	881	125	14.2	9	1.1	116	13.1	756	85.8	565	64.2	191	21.6
25–29 years	1,365	98	7.2	10	0.7	88	6.4	1,268	92.8	996	73.0	271	19.9
30–34 years	1,185	95	8.0	8	0.7	87	7.4	1,090	92.0	880	74.2	210	17.7

Appendix Table A-23, Continued

Age, Sex, Race, Spanish Origin, and Mexican Origin	Population	Enrolled in School						Not Enrolled in School					
		Total		Below College Level[1]		In College		Total		High-School Graduate		Not High-School Graduate	
	Number	Number	Percentage	Number	Percentage	Number	Percentage	Number	Percentage	Number	Percentage	Number	Percentage
SPANISH ORIGIN[2]													
Total, 3–34 years	9,359	4,617	49.3	4,095	43.8	523	5.6	4,741	50.7	2,202	23.5	2,539	27.1
3–4 years	642	151	23.5	151	23.5	—	—	491	76.5	—	—	491	76.5
5–6 years	593	564	95.1	564	95.1	—	—	29	4.9	—	—	29	4.9
7–9 years	894	880	98.5	880	98.5	—	—	14	1.5	—	—	14	1.5
10–13 years	1,263	1,259	99.7	1,259	99.7	—	—	4	0.3	—	—	4	0.3
14–15 years	616	591	96.0	591	96.0	—	—	25	4.0	—	—	25	4.0
16–17 years	561	498	88.6	480	85.6	17	3.1	64	11.4	6	1.1	58	10.2
18–19 years	573	254	44.3	120	20.9	134	23.4	319	55.7	154	26.8	166	28.9
20–21 years	614	147	24.0	23	3.7	124	20.2	467	76.0	232	37.7	235	38.3
22–24 years	838	105	12.5	13	1.6	91	10.9	733	87.5	375	44.8	358	42.7
25–29 years	1,468	120	8.2	6	0.4	114	7.8	1,348	91.8	746	50.8	602	41.0
30–34 years	1,296	49	3.8	8	0.6	41	3.2	1,247	96.2	689	53.1	558	43.1
Male, 3-to 34 years	4,626	2,347	50.7	2,094	45.3	253	5.5	2,279	49.3	1,008	21.8	1,271	27.5
3–4 years	329	82	25.0	82	25.0	—	—	247	75.0	—	—	247	75.0
5–6 years	302	278	91.9	278	91.9	—	—	24	8.1	—	—	24	8.1
7–9 years	464	459	98.8	459	98.8	—	—	5	1.2	—	—	5	1.2
10–13 years	631	628	99.6	628	99.6	—	—	2	0.4	—	—	2	0.4
14–15 years	321	313	97.8	313	97.8	—	—	7	2.2	—	—	7	2.2
16–17 years	273	240	88.2	230	84.5	10	3.7	32	11.8	3	1.2	29	10.7
18–19 years	266	108	40.4	67	25.1	41	15.3	159	59.6	72	27.0	87	32.6
20–21 years	311	82	26.2	21	6.7	61	19.5	230	73.8	95	30.6	134	43.2
22–24 years	391	59	15.1	9	2.4	50	12.7	332	84.9	157	40.1	175	44.7
25–29 years	729	78	10.8	4	0.6	74	10.2	651	89.2	358	49.2	292	40.1
30–34 years	608	19	3.1	2	0.3	17	2.8	589	96.9	322	52.9	267	44.0
Female, 3–34 years	4,733	2,271	48.0	2,001	42.3	270	5.7	2,462	52.0	1,194	25.2	1,268	26.8
3–4 years	313	69	22.0	69	22.0	—	—	244	78.0	—	—	244	78.0
5–6 years	291	286	98.3	286	98.3	—	—	5	1.7	—	—	5	1.7
7–9 years	430	421	98.1	421	98.1	—	—	8	1.9	—	—	8	1.9
10–13 years	632	631	99.8	631	99.8	—	—	1	0.2	—	—	1	0.2
14–15 years	295	278	94.1	278	94.1	—	—	18	5.9	—	—	18	5.9
16–17 years	289	257	89.1	250	86.6	7	2.5	32	10.9	3	1.1	28	9.8
18–19 years	307	146	47.6	53	17.2	93	30.4	161	52.4	82	26.7	79	25.6
20–21 years	303	66	21.7	2	0.7	64	21.0	237	78.3	136	45.1	101	33.3
22–24 years	447	45	10.1	4	0.9	41	9.3	401	89.9	218	48.9	183	41.0
25–29 years	739	42	5.7	2	0.3	40	5.4	698	94.3	388	52.4	310	41.9
30–34 years	688	30	4.4	6	0.8	25	3.6	657	95.6	367	53.3	291	42.3

MEXICAN ORIGIN[2]

Total, 3–34 years	6,333	3,098	48.9	2,831	44.7	267	4.2	3,235	51.1	1,368	21.6	1,868	29.5
3–4 years	463	90	19.4	90	19.4	—	—	373	80.6	—	—	373	80.6
5–6 years	402	385	95.9	385	95.9	—	—	17	4.1	—	—	17	4.1
7–9 years	651	643	98.8	643	98.8	—	—	8	1.2	—	—	8	1.2
10–13 years	875	873	99.7	873	99.7	—	—	2	0.3	—	—	2	0.3
14–15 years	434	410	94.3	410	94.3	—	1.5	25	5.7	—	—	25	5.7
16–17 years	374	329	88.1	324	86.6	6	16.9	45	11.9	3	0.7	42	11.2
18–19 years	361	137	37.9	76	21.0	61	15.8	224	62.1	107	29.6	117	32.5
20–21 years	396	73	18.5	11	2.8	62	9.7	323	81.5	148	37.4	175	44.1
22–24 years	562	62	11.1	8	1.4	54	6.2	499	88.9	230	41.0	269	48.0
25–29 years	943	64	6.8	6	0.6	58	2.9	878	93.2	442	46.9	437	46.3
30–34 years	874	32	3.6	6	0.7	26		842	96.4	439	50.2	403	46.2
Male, 3–34 years	3,158	1,582	50.1	1,456	46.1	125	4.0	1,576	49.9	614	19.4	962	30.5
3–4 years	238	49	20.4	49	20.4	—	—	190	79.6	—	—	190	79.6
5–6 years	208	196	94.4	196	94.4	—	—	12	5.6	—	—	12	5.6
7–9 years	338	333	98.4	333	98.4	—	—	5	1.6	—	—	5	1.6
10–13 years	442	440	99.5	440	99.5	—	—	2	0.5	—	—	2	0.5
14–15 years	235	228	96.9	228	96.9	—	—	7	3.1	—	—	7	3.1
16–17 years	178	154	86.2	152	85.3	2	1.0	25	13.8	1	0.5	24	13.3
18–19 years	164	59	35.8	40	24.2	19	11.6	105	64.2	43	26.3	62	37.9
20–21 years	193	32	16.6	9	4.6	23	11.9	161	83.4	59	30.5	102	53.0
22–24 years	259	40	15.6	4	1.5	36	14.0	219	84.4	91	35.0	128	49.4
25–29 years	481	38	7.9	4	0.9	34	7.1	443	92.1	218	45.4	225	46.7
30–34 years	422	13	3.2	2	0.5	11	2.7	408	96.8	203	48.1	206	48.8
Female, 3–34 years	3,176	1,517	47.8	1,375	43.3	142	4.5	1,659	52.2	754	23.7	906	28.5
3–4 years	225	41	18.4	41	18.4	—	—	184	81.6	—	—	184	81.6
5–6 years	194	189	97.4	189	97.4	—	—	5	2.6	—	—	5	2.6
7–9 years	313	310	99.3	310	99.3	—	—	2	0.7	—	—	2	0.7
10–13 years	433	433	100.0	433	100.0	—	—	—	—	—	—	—	—
14–15 years	199	182	91.2	182	91.2	—	—	18	8.8	—	—	18	8.8
16–17 years	196	175	89.7	172	87.8	4	1.9	20	10.3	2	0.9	18	9.3
18–19 years	197	78	39.7	36	18.4	42	21.3	119	60.3	64	32.3	55	28.0
20–21 years	203	41	20.4	2	1.0	39	19.4	162	79.6	89	44.0	72	35.6
22–24 years	303	22	7.2	4	1.3	18	6.0	281	92.8	139	46.0	141	46.8
25–29 years	462	26	5.6	2	0.4	24	5.2	436	94.4	224	48.4	212	45.9
30–34 years	452	18	4.1	4	0.9	14	3.2	434	95.9	236	52.2	198	43.8

1 Includes nursery school, kindergarten, and grades 1 to 12.

2 Persons of Spanish origin may be of any race.

Source: *Current Population Reports*, P-20, no. 413, table 1, pp. 9–11.

* Numbers in thousands. Civilian noninstitutional population.

A-24 Attendance Status, for College Students 16–34 Years Old, by Sex, Age, Residence, Year, and Control of College, Race, and Spanish Origin: October 1983

Year and Control of College, Age, Residence, Race, and Spanish Origin	Both Sexes			Male			Female		
	Total Enrolled	Attending Full-Time		Total Enrolled	Attending Full-Time		Total Enrolled	Attending Full-Time	
		Number	Percentage		Number	Percentage		Number	Percentage
ALL RACES									
Total, 16–34 years old	10,817	7,703	71.2	5,502	4,038	73.4	5,315	3,665	69.0
16–17 years old	252	226	89.7	106	93	88.1	147	133	90.9
18–19 years old	2,940	2,661	90.5	1,340	1,208	90.2	1,600	1,452	90.8
20–21 years old	2,495	2,155	86.4	1,310	1,139	87.0	1,185	1,016	85.7
22–24 years old	2,042	1,412	69.2	1,170	854	73.0	872	558	64.0
25–29 years old	1,921	859	44.7	1,055	540	51.1	865	319	36.9
30–34 years old	1,167	390	33.4	521	204	39.0	645	186	28.9
College year									
First	2,980	2,104	70.6	1,380	975	70.6	1,600	1,130	70.6
Second	2,624	1,959	74.7	1,315	1,017	77.3	1,309	942	72.0
Third	1,805	1,378	76.3	919	708	77.0	886	670	75.6
Fourth	1,595	1,281	80.3	871	715	82.1	723	565	78.1
Fifth	850	437	51.5	467	289	61.8	383	149	38.9
Sixth or higher	964	544	56.4	550	334	60.8	414	210	50.6
Residence									
Metropolitan:	8,273	5,732	69.3	4,264	3,038	70.7	4,009	2,694	67.2
In central city	3,395	2,331	68.7	1,760	1,249	71.0	1,635	1,082	66.2
Outside central city	4,878	3,401	69.7	2,504	1,789	71.5	2,374	1,612	67.9
Nonmetropolitan	2,545	1,972	77.5	1,239	1,000	80.7	1,306	972	74.4
Control of college									
Public	8,177	5,686	69.5	4,110	2,951	71.8	4,068	2,735	67.2
Private	2,640	2,017	76.4	1,393	1,087	78.1	1,247	930	74.6
WHITE									
Total, 16–34 years old	9,236	6,526	70.7	4,717	3,450	73.1	4,520	3,076	68.1
16–17 years old	208	191	91.7	85	77	90.5	123	113	92.5
18–19 years old	2,597	2,366	91.1	1,197	1,090	91.0	1,400	1,276	91.1
20–21 years old	2,161	1,863	86.2	1,149	1,000	87.0	1,012	863	85.3
22–24 years old	1,705	1,149	67.4	989	710	71.8	717	439	61.3
25–29 years old	1,603	658	41.0	875	414	47.3	728	243	33.4
30–34 years old	961	300	31.2	421	158	37.7	540	142	26.2

College year									
First	2,505	1,779	71.0	1,152	831	72.2	1,353	948	70.1
Second	2,217	1,660	74.9	1,115	863	77.4	1,103	797	72.3
Third	1,553	1,159	74.6	802	608	75.8	751	551	73.4
Fourth	1,384	1,111	80.3	765	626	81.7	618	485	78.4
Fifth	732	351	47.9	395	226	57.2	337	125	37.0
Sixth or higher	845	467	55.2	488	296	60.7	358	170	47.6
Residence									
Metropolitan:	6,943	4,769	68.7	3,599	2,553	70.9	3,345	2,216	66.2
In central city	2,541	1,693	66.6	1,345	930	69.1	1,196	763	63.8
Outside central city	4,402	3,076	69.9	2,254	1,623	72.0	2,149	1,453	67.6
Nonmetropolitan	2,293	1,757	76.6	1,118	896	80.2	1,175	860	73.2
Control of college									
Public	6,943	4,778	68.8	3,501	2,510	71.7	3,442	2,268	65.9
Private	2,293	1,748	76.2	1,215	939	77.3	1,078	809	75.0
BLACK									
Total, 16–34 years old	1,102	806	73.1	497	361	72.5	605	446	73.7
16–17 years old	31	23	(B)	12	8	(B)	19	15	(B)
18–19 years old	258	226	87.7	93	79	84.3	164	147	89.6
20–21 years old	242	210	86.5	112	96	86.5	131	113	86.6
22–24 years old	241	186	77.2	126	101	80.0	116	86	74.1
25–29 years old	179	100	55.9	91	54	59.7	88	46	51.9
30–34 years old	151	61	40.5	64	22	(B)	87	39	44.5
College year									
First	355	242	68.2	149	87	58.7	206	155	75.2
Second	302	217	71.9	141	105	74.3	161	112	69.7
Third	185	162	87.4	85	73	85.8	101	89	88.7
Fourth	150	115	76.7	74	62	(B)	76	53	70.6
Fifth	54	34	(B)	28	21	(B)	26	13	(B)
Sixth or higher	56	36	(B)	20	13	(B)	36	23	(B)
Residence									
Metropolitan:	945	676	71.5	430	305	70.9	514	371	72.2
In central city	659	489	74.3	303	227	75.1	356	262	73.6
Outside central city	286	187	65.5	127	78	61.4	158	109	68.8
Nonmetropolitan	158	130	82.2	67	55	(B)	90	75	82.5
Control of college									
Public	858	617	71.9	388	266	68.7	470	350	74.6
Private	245	189	77.4	109	94	86.1	135	95	70.3
SPANISH ORIGIN[1]									
Total, 16–34 years old	523	335	64.0	253	149	59.0	270	186	68.7

Numbers in thousands. Civilian noninstitutional population.

1 Persons of Spanish origin may be of any race.

Source: *Current Population Reports*, P-20, no. 413, table 6, p. 23.

A-25 School Enrollment of Persons 3–34 Years Old, by Level and Control of School, Race, and Spanish Origin: October 1960–1985

Level and Control of School	1985	1984	1983	1982	1981¹	1981²	1980	1979	1978	1977	1976	1975	1970	1965	1960
ALL RACES															
Total enrolled	58,014	57,313	57,745	57,905	58,390	56,940	57,348	57,854	58,616	60,013	60,482	60,969	60,357	54,701	[5]46,260
Nursery school	2,491	2,354	2,350	2,153	2,058	2,026	1,987	1,869	1,824	1,618	1,526	1,748	1,096	520	(NA)
Public	854	761	809	729	663	657	633	636	587	562	476	574	333	127	(NA)
Private	1,637	1,593	1,541	1,423	1,396	1,369	1,354	1,233	1,237	1,056	1,050	1,174	763	393	(NA)
Kindergarten	3,815	3,484	3,361	3,229	3,161	3,069	3,176	3,025	2,989	3,191	3,490	3,393	3,183	3,057	2,092
Public	3,221	2,953	2,706	2,746	2,616	2,540	2,690	2,593	2,493	2,665	2,962	2,851	2,647	2,439	1,691
Private	594	531	656	553	545	529	486	432	496	526	528	542	536	618	401
Elementary school	26,866	26,838	27,198	27,412	27,795	27,059	27,449	27,865	28,490	29,234	29,774	30,446	33,950	32,474	30,349
Public	23,803	24,120	24,203	24,381	24,758	24,083	24,398	24,756	25,252	25,983	26,698	27,166	30,001	27,596	25,814
Private	3,063	2,718	2,994	3,031	3,037	2,976	3,051	3,109	3,238	3,251	3,075	3,279	3,949	4,878	4,535
High school	13,979	13,777	14,010	14,123	14,642	14,349	14,556	15,116	15,475	15,753	15,742	15,683	14,715	12,975	10,249
Public	12,764	12,721	12,792	13,004	13,523	13,249	(NA)	13,994	14,231	14,505	14,541	14,503	13,545	11,517	9,215
Private	1,215	1,057	1,218	1,118	1,119	1,100	(NA)	1,122	1,244	1,248	1,201	1,180	1,170	1,457	1,033
College	10,863	10,859	10,825	10,919	10,734	10,437	10,180	9,978	9,838	10,217	9,950	9,697	7,413	5,675	3,570
Public	8,379	8,467	8,183	8,354	8,159	7,911	(NA)	7,699	7,427	7,925	7,739	7,704	5,699	3,840	2,307
Private	2,483	2,392	2,640	2,565	2,576	2,525	(NA)	2,280	2,410	2,292	2,211	1,994	1,714	1,835	1,262
College															
Full time	7,720	7,822	7,711	7,736	7,569	7,384	7,147	7,010	6,979	7,196	7,176	7,105	5,763	4,414	2,681
Percentage	71.1	72.0	71.2	70.8	70.5	70.7	70.2	70.3	70.9	70.4	72.1	73.3	77.7	77.8	75.1
Part time	3,143	3,037	3,114	3,183	3,166	3,053	3,033	2,968	2,859	3,021	2,773	2,592	1,650	1,261	887
WHITE															
Total enrolled	47,452	46,941	47,423	47,662	48,169	47,098	47,673	48,225	48,843	50,151	50,761	51,430	51,719	47,451	[5]40,348
Nursery school	2,087	1,915	1,932	1,783	1,685	1,657	1,637	1,537	1,456	1,314	1,246	1,432	893	451	(NA)
Public	617	543	563	504	447	441	432	428	351	372	318	392	198	93	(NA)
Private	1,470	1,372	1,369	1,279	1,238	1,216	1,205	1,110	1,105	942	929	1,040	695	358	(NA)
Kindergarten	3,060	2,788	2,769	2,677	2,597	2,514	2,595	2,437	2,452	2,611	2,881	2,845	2,706	2,648	1,849
Public	2,545	2,319	2,181	2,189	2,130	2,060	2,172	2,069	2,009	2,153	2,423	2,363	2,233	2,086	1,485
Private	515	469	588	489	467	453	423	368	444	458	457	483	473	562	364
Elementary school	21,593	21,730	22,054	22,297	22,663	22,081	22,510	22,959	23,524	24,262	24,776	25,412	28,638	27,679	26,035
Public	18,817	19,282	19,340	19,583	19,924	19,390	19,743	20,174	20,551	21,312	21,947	22,351	24,923	22,976	21,696
Private	2,776	2,449	2,714	2,713	2,739	2,691	2,768	2,785	2,973	2,950	2,829	3,059	3,715	4,703	4,339
High school	11,378	11,240	11,425	11,577	12,062	11,862	12,056	12,583	12,897	13,152	13,214	13,224	12,723	11,356	9,122
Public	10,258	10,266	10,339	10,541	11,035	10,849	(NA)	11,549	11,741	11,980	12,093	12,112	11,599	9,961	8,124
Private	1,120	974	1,086	1,036	1,027	1,013	(NA)	1,033	1,156	1,172	1,121	1,112	1,124	1,395	999
College	9,334	9,269	9,242	9,328	9,162	8,983	8,875	8,709	8,514	8,812	8,644	8,526	6,759	5,317	3,342
Public	7,131	7,163	6,949	7,102	6,906	6,754	(NA)	6,672	6,368	6,743	6,657	6,724	5,168	3,568	2,126
Private	2,203	2,105	2,293	2,227	2,256	2,229	(NA)	2,037	2,145	2,069	1,987	1,792	1,591	1,749	1,215

College															
Full time	6,597	6,672	6,532	6,579	6,452	6,349	6,212	6,058	5,974	6,165	6,170	6,183	5,221	4,111	(NA)
Percentage	70.7	72.0	70.7	70.5	70.4	70.7	70.0	69.6	70.2	70.0	71.4	72.6	77.2	77.3	(NA)
BLACK															
Total enrolled	8,444	8,226	8,199	8,262	8,350	8,282	8,251	8,317	8,416	8,564	8,518	8,400	7,829	[4]7,252	[4,5]5,910
Nursery school	332	340	326	305	284	294	294	278	312	250	226	276	178	72	(NA)
Public	212	179	215	192	182	187	180	185	210	171	146	171	129	37	(NA)
Private	120	161	111	113	102	107	115	95	102	78	80	105	49	35	(NA)
Kindergarten	625	563	476	508	474	477	490	497	451	496	542	468	426	407	243
Public	562	513	427	463	412	415	440	443	414	447	482	426	374	353	206
Private	63	61	48	45	62	62	50	54	38	50	60	42	53	54	37
Elementary school	4,307	4,123	4,153	4,194	4,291	4,281	4,259	4,296	4,356	4,387	4,430	4,509	4,868	4,796	4,313
Public	4,131	3,947	3,964	3,974	4,087	4,072	4,058	4,053	4,154	4,166	4,256	4,344	4,668	4,620	4,118
Private	175	177	189	220	204	208	202	243	202	221	175	165	200	176	195
High school	2,131	2,061	2,143	2,128	2,168	2,150	2,200	2,245	2,276	2,327	2,258	2,199	1,834	1,619	1,127
Public	2,068	2,002	2,057	2,073	2,102	2,085	(NA)	2,172	2,211	2,269	2,187	2,140	1,794	1,556	1,092
Private	63	59	86	55	65	65	(NA)	74	65	59	71	59	41	62	34
College	1,049	1,138	1,102	1,127	1,133	1,080	1,007	1,002	1,020	1,103	1,062	948	522	358	227
Public	860	918	858	865	898	857	(NA)	814	822	916	887	782	422	272	180
Private	190	220	245	263	235	223	(NA)	188	199	187	175	166	100	86	46
College															
Full time	767	810	806	800	815	776	723	748	753	803	817	742	427	218	(NA)
Percentage	73.1	71.2	73.1	71.0	71.9	71.9	71.8	74.6	73.8	72.8	76.9	78.3	81.8	79.6	(NA)
SPANISH ORIGIN[3]															
Total enrolled	5,070	4,284	4,618	4,478	4,551	4,378	4,263	3,608	3,455	3,516	3,623	3,741	(NA)	(NA)	(NA)
Nursery school	168	117	108	83	131	126	146	89	87	75	68	85	(NA)	(NA)	(NA)
Public	105	78	60	46	68	66	70	50	47	30	38	47	(NA)	(NA)	(NA)
Private	63	39	48	37	63	60	75	39	39	46	30	39	(NA)	(NA)	(NA)
Kindergarten	364	293	335	329	306	292	263	226	231	220	262	235	(NA)	(NA)	(NA)
Public	315	267	285	291	282	268	234	210	198	206	242	218	(NA)	(NA)	(NA)
Private	49	26	50	37	24	23	30	16	33	14	20	17	(NA)	(NA)	(NA)
Elementary school	2,803	2,384	2,548	2,501	2,474	2,373	2,363	1,934	1,893	1,874	1,934	2,062	(NA)	(NA)	(NA)
Public	2,607	2,218	2,323	2,276	2,239	2,146	2,134	1,745	1,704	1,654	1,768	1,858	(NA)	(NA)	(NA)
Private	196	166	225	225	235	227	228	189	188	220	165	204	(NA)	(NA)	(NA)
High school	1,156	966	1,104	1,072	1,130	1,101	1,048	920	868	928	932	948	(NA)	(NA)	(NA)
Public	1,090	909	1,027	995	1,056	1,029	(NA)	875	825	836	867	886	(NA)	(NA)	(NA)
Private	67	57	77	77	74	72	(NA)	45	43	92	65	61	(NA)	(NA)	(NA)
College	579	524	523	493	510	486	443	440	377	418	427	411	(NA)	(NA)	(NA)
Public	464	433	441	398	398	379	(NA)	365	315	357	354	358	(NA)	(NA)	(NA)
Private	116	91	82	96	112	107	(NA)	75	62	60	73	53	(NA)	(NA)	(NA)
College															
Full time	381	356	335	312	343	326	295	314	231	287	297	287	(NA)	(NA)	(NA)
Percentage	65.8	67.9	64.1	63.3	67.3	67.1	66.4	71.4	61.3	68.7	69.6	69.8	(NA)	(NA)	(NA)

Numbers in thousands. Civilian noninstitutional population.

1 Controlled to 1980 census base.

2 Controlled to 1970 census base.

3 Persons of Spanish origin may be of any race.

4 Enrollment figures for 1960 and 1965 are for black and other races.

5 Enrollment figures for 1960 are for the population 5–34 years old.

Source: *Current Population Reports,* P-20, no. 409, table 1, p. 4.

Enrollment in Public Elementary and Secondary Schools, by Race/Ethnicity and State: Fall 1984

State	Percent of Enrollment, by Race/Ethnicity				
	Total	White[1]	Black[1]	Hispanic	Asian or Pacific Islander	American Indian/ Alaskan Native
United States	100.0	71.2	16.2	9.1	2.5	0.9
Alabama	100.0	63.9	34.5	0.1	0.3	1.1
Alaska	100.0	74.5	3.4	1.4	2.4	18.3
Arizona	100.0	62.3	3.8	21.5	1.1	11.3
Arkansas	100.0	73.9	25.3	0.3	0.5	0.1
California	100.0	52.0	10.1	29.2	8.1	0.6
Colorado	100.0	76.5	5.1	15.7	2.1	0.6
Connecticut	100.0	81.4	10.3	6.8	1.4	0.2
Delaware	100.0	70.7	25.8	2.1	1.2	0.1
District of Columbia	100.0	3.8	92.5	2.9	0.8	(2)
Florida	100.0	67.7	23.1	8.1	1.0	0.1
Georgia	100.0	63.0	35.8	0.4	0.8	(2)
Hawaii	100.0	23.1	1.9	2.1	72.7	0.3
Idaho	100.0	93.5	0.4	3.8	0.9	1.4
Illinois	100.0	64.7	24.8	8.0	2.3	0.1
Indiana	100.0	86.9	10.7	1.7	0.6	0.1
Iowa	100.0	96.0	1.8	1.0	1.0	0.2
Kansas	100.0	88.1	6.8	2.9	1.5	0.7
Kentucky	100.0	88.9	10.6	0.1	0.3	(2)
Louisiana	100.0	55.5	42.5	0.8	1.1	0.1
Maine	100.0	98.7	0.4	0.2	0.6	0.2
Maryland	100.0	58.2	37.2	1.5	3.0	0.2
Massachusetts	100.0	86.5	6.3	5.0	2.0	0.1
Michigan	100.0	79.5	16.7	1.9	0.8	1.0
Minnesota	100.0	93.4	2.4	0.9	2.0	1.3
Mississippi	100.0	49.3	50.4	0.1	0.1	0.1

State	Percent of Enrollment, by Race/Ethnicity					
	Total	White[1]	Black	Hispanic	Asian or Pacific Islander	American Indian/ Alaskan Native
Missouri	100.0	82.2	16.2	0.8	0.7	0.1
Montana	100.0	85.4	0.3	1.0	0.5	12.8
Nebraska	100.0	92.5	4.3	2.0	0.8	0.5
Nevada	100.0	78.3	9.9	6.6	2.9	2.3
New Hampshire	100.0	98.3	0.6	0.4	0.6	(²)
New Jersey	100.0	69.7	18.8	8.8	2.6	0.1
New Mexico	100.0	44.9	2.2	43.4	0.7	8.7
New York	100.0	64.4	18.7	13.6	3.2	0.1
North Carolina	100.0	66.2	30.0	0.3	0.6	2.9
North Dakota	100.0	92.4	0.5	0.5	0.7	5.8
Ohio	100.0	83.8	14.4	1.1	0.6	0.1
Oklahoma	100.0	76.4	9.9	2.0	1.2	10.6
Oregon	100.0	90.5	2.1	3.5	2.7	1.2
Pennsylvania	100.0	84.6	12.6	1.6	1.1	0.1
Rhode Island	100.0	88.5	5.5	3.8	2.0	0.3
South Carolina	100.0	58.6	40.6	0.2	0.5	0.2
South Dakota	100.0	92.5	0.5	0.4	0.7	6.0
Tennessee	100.0	78.5	20.9	0.1	0.5	(²)
Texas	100.0	56.6	13.9	27.9	1.4	0.1
Utah	100.0	93.4	0.5	3.3	1.8	1.0
Vermont	100.0	98.9	0.4	0.1	0.5	0.1
Virginia	100.0	72.4	23.8	1.1	2.6	0.1
Washington	100.0	85.5	3.8	4.3	4.7	1.8
West Virginia	100.0	95.4	4.2	0.1	0.3	(²)
Wisconsin	100.0	88.7	7.7	1.7	1.1	0.9
Wyoming	100.0	90.3	0.9	6.4	0.7	1.8

1 Excludes persons of Hispanic origin.

2 Less than 0.05 percent.

Source: *Digest of Education Statistics, 1987*, table 35, p. 46.

Enrollment in Public Elementary and Secondary Schools, by Grade and State: Fall 1985[1]

State or Other Area	Total, All Levels	Prekindergarten Through	
		Total	Prekinder-garten
United States	39,513,379	27,046,873	153,193
Alabama	730,460	517,361	—
Alaska	107,345	77,211	739
Arizona	548,252	386,057	—
Arkansas	433,410	303,536	—
California	4,255,554	2,926,705	—
Colorado	550,642	378,735	1,649
Connecticut	462,026	321,203	3,410
Delaware	92,901	63,082	287
District of Columbia	87,092	62,494	3,309
Florida	1,562,872	1,086,250	3,365
Georgia	1,079,594	756,752	—
Hawaii	164,169	111,564	270
Idaho	208,669	149,380	—
Illinois	1,826,478	1,246,496	21,185
Indiana	966,106	654,061	507
Iowa	485,332	324,332	974
Kansas	410,229	285,671	—
Kentucky	643,833	448,768	—
Louisiana	792,704	571,321	2,900
Maine	206,101	140,413	504
Maryland	671,560	446,321	8,710
Massachusetts	844,330	559,057	3,127
Michigan	1,689,828	1,103,969	7,956
Minnesota	705,140	467,957	5,205
Mississippi	471,195	329,981	—
Missouri	795,104	544,197	—
Montana	153,869	107,918	208
Nebraska	265,819	184,296	1,280
Nevada	154,948	107,070	—
New Hampshire	160,974	106,912	—
New Jersey	1,116,194	740,497	6,029
New Mexico	277,551	187,479	—
New York	2,621,378	1,703,430	16,015
North Carolina	1,086,165	749,451	—
North Dakota	118,570	83,702	605
Ohio	1,793,775	1,206,138	—
Oklahoma	592,327	414,279	2,271
Oregon	447,527	305,418	1,059
Pennsylvania	1,683,221	1,092,558	—
Rhode Island	133,442	89,958	369
South Carolina	606,643	424,125	—
South Dakota	124,291	87,644	416
Tennessee	813,753	574,517	926
Texas	3,131,705	2,260,679	44,888
Utah	403,395	298,760	—

Grade 8 and Elementary Unclassified

Kinder-garten	Grade 1	Grade 2	Grade 3	Grade 4
3,037,577	3,238,539	2,940,400	2,893,509	2,769,917
53,595	62,215	56,362	58,953	53,783
9,673	10,210	8,856	8,599	8,076
45,323	48,414	42,870	42,217	39,379
33,650	36,267	32,839	32,772	31,965
360,210	350,046	325,825	320,083	308,202
44,672	45,856	41,821	40,862	39,645
35,860	37,313	33,078	32,032	31,022
7,532	8,674	6,837	6,561	6,238
6,602	7,840	6,887	6,657	5,967
122,307	127,756	112,346	113,650	111,950
84,643	92,440	83,761	81,792	78,856
13,425	13,310	12,570	12,404	11,864
17,145	18,704	17,468	16,938	16,215
141,773	144,162	132,258	130,127	123,605
72,140	77,662	70,832	69,366	66,451
40,925	38,110	35,387	34,508	32,977
36,229	33,752	31,410	30,992	29,239
49,961	55,543	49,770	48,954	46,334
64,715	73,555	63,382	62,088	58,563
16,833	16,780	15,367	14,580	14,364
48,057	53,071	48,372	47,830	44,812
65,021	65,008	58,907	57,206	55,853
131,430	122,548	112,976	108,804	104,377
59,184	55,809	51,979	49,909	47,753
,683	44,890	39,743	39,934	36,822
63,128	64,886	60,148	58,726	55,284
12,942	13,003	12,333	11,975	11,445
23,418	21,781	20,337	20,028	18,957
12,464	13,278	12,093	11,866	11,255
5,290	15,353	11,899	11,389	10,964
77,160	83,353	76,910	76,373	73,133
22,617	23,751	21,790	20,731	19,604
178,484	199,595	184,866	179,091	173,322
80,743	84,005	79,842	79,789	76,002
10,081	10,299	9,571	9,406	8,870
142,344	146,091	131,048	128,629	125,200
48,660	52,730	45,590	44,800	42,140
25,979	38,576	35,144	34,826	33,462
121,985	129,118	115,359	111,603	107,751
9,636	11,162	9,427	9,197	8,866
41,117	53,124	46,172	46,687	44,270
11,119	10,885	9,901	9,667	9,214
58,255	68,606	61,329	60,718	58,126
241,272	279,290	249,249	245,553	237,283
38,731	37,582	33,628	35,330	33,418

(Continued)

Appendix Table A-27, Continued

State or Other Area	Total, All Levels	Prekindergarten Through	
		Total	Prekinder-garten
Vermont	90,157	62,703	218
Virginia	968,104	665,151	1,728
Washington	749,706	506,890	1,918
West Virginia	357,923	249,034	485
Wisconsin	768,234	501,402	10,681
Wyoming	102,779	73,988	—
Outlying areas			
Guam	26,043	19,266	380
Puerto Rico	686,894	507,973	—
Virgin Islands	25,386	18,599	—

State or Other Area	Prekindergarten Through Grade 8 and Elementary Unclassified				
	Grade 5	Grade 6	Grade 7	Grade 8	Elementary Unclassified
United States	2,774,737	2,787,067	2,936,146	2,979,474	536,314
Alabama	55,181	56,714	61,480	59,078	—
Alaska	7,689	7,603	7,964	7,802	—
Arizona	39,234	39,178	40,984	41,981	6,477
Arkansas	31,937	32,600	34,183	35,066	2,257
California	303,277	299,902	304,180	307,778	47,202
Colorado	39,401	38,802	40,604	41,793	3,630
Connecticut	31,065	31,302	32,463	34,336	19,322
Delaware	6,456	6,228	7,010	7,259	—
District of Columbia	5,806	5,459	6,505	5,959	1,503
Florida	115,057	119,983	129,701	130,135	—
Georgia	79,236	80,068	84,221	79,611	12,124
Hawaii	11,157	11,124	10,645	10,729	4,066
Idaho	15,644	15,558	15,434	15,305	969
Illinois	123,338	122,975	125,118	130,507	51,448
Indiana	67,851	67,239	72,766	75,450	13,797
Iowa	33,237	32,038	32,653	35,136	8,387
Kansas	28,850	28,221	29,508	30,246	7,224
Kentucky	45,942	44,173	48,402	51,083	8,606
Louisiana	56,486	53,585	60,173	54,824	21,050
Maine	14,659	14,871	15,901	16,554	—
Maryland	44,874	45,527	48,583	51,196	5,289
Massachusetts	56,738	58,556	62,165	65,666	10,810
Michigan	106,597	109,768	115,120	119,123	65,270
Minnesota	48,394	47,198	50,073	52,453	—
Mississippi	36,688	34,960	39,528	38,036	7,697
Missouri	56,013	56,081	59,464	61,456	9,011
Montana	11,128	10,708	10,990	11,400	1,786
Nebraska	19,824	19,181	19,202	20,288	—
Nevada	10,853	10,949	11,452	11,964	896
New Hampshire	11,245	11,789	12,356	13,500	3,127
New Jersey	74,412	74,858	78,494	81,086	38,689
New Mexico	19,711	19,406	19,955	19,914	—
New York	170,467	171,290	184,313	182,211	63,773
North Carolina	78,692	81,778	87,006	89,062	12,532
North Dakota	8,599	8,511	8,960	8,800	—

Grade 8 and Elementary Unclassified

Kinder-garten	Grade 1	Grade 2	Grade 3	Grade 4
6,496	7,986	7,002	6,745	6,541
73,699	77,248	69,400	68,911	65,704
61,026	62,668	56,924	56,117	52,959
26,697	26,383	26,734	26,759	25,429
62,068	58,482	53,467	52,528	48,595
9,578	9,366	8,334	8,247	7,811
2,163	2,253	2,210	2,149	1,993
32,120	64,081	60,058	59,824	59,558
1,839	2,008	1,951	1,936	1,896

Grades 9 Through 12 and Secondary Unclassified

Total	Grade 9	Grade 10	Grade 11	Grade 12	Secondary Unclassified
12,466,506	3,438,189	3,229,292	2,867,044	2,550,014	381,967
213,099	64,173	55,635	49,665	43,626	—
30,134	8,774	7,924	6,955	6,481	—
162,195	46,009	42,780	37,976	34,297	1,133
129,874	35,875	33,989	30,567	28,201	1,242
1,328,849	363,733	367,941	325,690	243,398	28,087
171,907	46,771	45,629	40,619	35,538	3,350
140,823	37,096	36,915	34,793	32,006	13
29,819	8,537	8,114	6,588	6,580	—
24,598	6,183	6,782	5,340	4,193	2,100
476,622	147,744	132,421	105,804	90,653	—
322,842	99,693	81,314	71,538	63,157	7,140
52,605	12,739	12,715	11,644	9,911	5,596
59,289	16,008	15,467	14,127	13,035	652
579,982	148,627	145,959	130,500	117,626	37,270
312,045	83,450	77,632	71,081	66,223	13,659
161,000	39,688	39,337	37,203	35,906	8,866
124,558	32,710	32,186	29,867	27,215	2,580
195,065	57,749	50,797	43,445	39,284	3,790
221,383	64,337	55,041	49,110	42,895	10,000
65,688	17,882	16,326	15,168	13,705	2,607
225,239	61,848	57,357	50,764	48,250	7,020
285,273	76,255	75,140	69,349	64,529	—
585,859	143,915	132,336	117,864	105,775	85,969
237,183	59,985	61,253	59,210	56,735	—
141,214	40,364	37,596	31,134	27,301	4,819
250,910	70,746	63,552	59,732	52,904	3,976
45,951	12,344	11,770	11,067	10,294	476
81,523	21,701	21,204	19,784	18,834	—
47,878	13,154	12,810	11,787	10,127	—
54,062	15,308	14,052	12,561	11,558	583
375,697	95,861	94,261	87,228	81,505	16,842
90,072	21,662	20,513	18,299	16,934	12,664
917,948	237,940	237,015	197,543	170,394	75,056
336,714	100,772	91,322	75,493	69,127	—
34,868	9,191	9,268	8,425	7,984	—

(Continued)

Appendix Table A-27, Continued

State or Other Area	Prekindergarten Through Grade 8 and Elementary Unclassified				
	Grade 5	Grade 6	Grade 7	Grade 8	Elementary Unclassified
Ohio	128,162	127,272	135,669	141,723	—
Oklahoma	40,355	42,887	44,055	45,121	5,670
Oregon	33,545	32,661	33,284	34,355	2,527
Pennsylvania	110,251	112,496	122,465	128,692	32,838
Rhode Island	8,804	9,103	10,086	10,328	2,980
South Carolina	45,113	46,856	49,879	50,907	—
South Dakota	8,981	8,489	8,657	9,153	1,162
Tennessee	59,329	60,814	64,769	64,768	16,877
Texas	235,204	238,336	248,818	240,786	—
Utah	30,482	29,571	28,595	26,790	4,633
Vermont	6,619	6,564	6,837	7,210	485
Virginia	65,997	67,600	72,773	76,495	25,596
Washington	52,703	52,963	53,707	55,905	—
West Virginia	25,897	26,180	29,000	28,513	6,957
Wisconsin	49,859	49,564	52,369	54,279	9,510
Wyoming	7,698	7,528	7,627	7,662	137
Outlying areas					
Guam	2,149	1,969	2,104	1,896	—
Puerto Rico	57,428	55,479	57,543	53,291	8,591
Virgin Islands	1,918	1,789	2,589	2,013	660

1   Preliminary data

—   Data not reported or not applicable

Source: *Digest of Education Statistics, 1987*, table 31, pp. 40–41.

	Grades 9 Through 12 and Secondary Unclassified				
Total	Grade 9	Grade 10	Grade 11	Grade 12	Secondary Unclassified
587,637	165,341	151,758	139,986	130,552	—
178,048	49,425	46,022	42,241	37,308	3,052
142,109	38,005	37,835	34,440	30,847	982
590,663	150,073	149,053	135,533	127,406	28,598
43,484	11,895	11,420	10,188	9,430	551
182,518	56,988	49,281	39,237	37,012	—
36,647	9,490	9,537	8,672	8,378	570
239,236	70,645	64,573	54,437	49,581	—
871,026	275,458	224,718	198,108	172,742	—
104,635	27,949	27,017	24,414	22,543	2,712
27,454	7,381	7,155	6,411	6,116	391
302,953	87,005	79,223	70,846	65.792	87
242,816	64,672	63,909	59,385	54,850	—
108,889	29,821	26,801	24,575	22,564	5,128
266,832	67,268	68,841	63,661	62,661	4,401
28,791	7,949	7,796	6,990	6,051	5
6,777	2,300	1,677	1,332	1,295	173
178,921	50,566	48,422	41,094	35,514	3,325
6,787	2,208	1,830	1,310	965	474

A-28 Public High-School Graduates, by State: 1969–70 to 1984–85

State	1969–70	1974–75	1979–80	1980–81	1981–82	1982–83	1983–84	1984–85	Percentage Change, 1979–80 to 1984–85
United States	2,588,639	2,822,638	2,747,678	2,725,285	2,710,837	2,597,744	¹2,501,165	²2,419,646	−11.9
Alabama	45,286	46,633	45,190	44,894	45,409	44,352	42,021	40,002	−11.5
Alaska	3,297	4,220	5,223	5,343	5,477	5,622	5,457	5,184	−0.7
Arizona	22,040	25,665	28,633	28,416	28,049	26,530	28,332	27,877	−2.6
Arkansas	26,068	26,836	29,052	29,577	29,710	28,447	27,049	26,342	−9.3
California	260,908	273,411	249,217	242,172	241,343	236,897	232,199	225,448	−9.5
Colorado	30,312	34,963	36,804	35,897	35,494	34,875	32,954	32,255	−12.4
Connecticut	34,755	42,792	37,683	38,369	37,706	36,204	33,679	32,126	−14.7
Delaware	6,985	8,235	7,582	7,349	7,144	6,924	6,410	5,893	−22.3
District of Columbia	4,980	5,367	4,959	4,848	4,521	4,909	³4,073	³3,940	−20.5
Florida	70,478	86,481	87,324	88,755	90,736	86,871	85,908	81,140	−7.1
Georgia	56,859	59,803	61,621	62,963	64,489	63,293	60,718	58,654	−4.8
Hawaii	10,407	11,283	11,493	11,472	11,563	10,757	10,454	10,092	−12.2
Idaho	12,296	12,631	13,187	12,679	12,560	12,126	11,732	12,148	−7.9
Illinois	126,864	141,316	135,579	136,795	136,534	128,814	122,561	117,027	−13.7
Indiana	69,984	74,104	73,143	73,381	73,984	70,549	65,710	63,308	−13.4
Iowa	44,063	43,005	43,445	42,635	41,509	39,569	37,248	36,087	−16.9
Kansas	33,394	32,458	30,890	29,397	28,298	28,316	26,730	25,983	−15.9
Kentucky	37,473	42,368	41,203	41,714	42,531	40,478	39,645	37,999	−7.8
Louisiana	43,641	47,691	46,297	46,199	46,324	39,539	39,400	39,460	−14.8
Maine	14,003	14,830	15,445	15,554	14,764	14,600	13,935	13,924	−9.8
Maryland	46,462	55,408	54,270	54,050	54,621	52,446	50,684	48,299	−11.0
Massachusetts	63,865	79,000	73,802	74,831	73,414	71,219	65,885	63,411	−14.1
Michigan	121,000	135,509	124,316	124,372	121,030	112,950	115,206	111,816	−10.1
Minnesota	60,480	66,535	64,908	64,166	62,145	59,015	55,376	53,352	−17.8
Mississippi	29,653	27,243	27,586	28,083	28,023	27,271	26,324	25,315	−8.2

State									% change
Missouri	55,315	62,375	62,265	60,359	59,872	56,420	53,388	51,290	−17.6
Montana	11,520	12,293	12,135	11,634	11,162	10,689	10,224	10,016	−17.5
Nebraska	21,280	22,249	22,410	21,027	21,411	19,986	18,674	18,036	−19.5
Nevada	5,449	7,232	8,473	9,069	9,240	8,979	8,726	8,572	1.2
New Hampshire	8,516	11,050	11,722	11,552	11,669	11,470	11,478	11,052	−5.7
New Jersey	86,498	96,000	94,564	93,168	93,750	90,048	85,569	81,547	−13.8
New Mexico	16,060	18,438	18,424	17,915	17,635	16,530	15,914	15,622	−15.2
New York	190,000	210,780	204,064	198,465	194,605	184,022	174,762	166,752	−18.3
North Carolina	68,886	70,094	70,862	69,395	71,210	68,783	66,803	67,245	−5.1
North Dakota	11,150	10,690	9,928	9,924	9,504	8,886	8,569	8,146	−17.9
Ohio	142,248	158,179	144,169	143,503	139,899	133,524	127,837	122,281	−15.2
Oklahoma	36,293	37,809	39,305	38,875	38,347	36,799	35,254	34,626	−11.9
Oregon	32,236	30,668	29,939	28,729	28,780	28,099	27,214	26,870	−10.3
Pennsylvania	151,014	163,124	146,458	144,645	143,356	137,494	132,412	127,226	−13.1
Rhode Island	10,146	11,042	10,864	10,719	10,545	10,533	9,652	9,201	−15.3
South Carolina	34,940	38,312	38,697	38,347	38,647	37,570	36,800	34,500	−10.8
South Dakota	11,757	11,725	10,689	10,385	9,864	9,206	8,638	8,206	−23.2
Tennessee	49,000	49,363	49,845	50,648	51,447	46,704	144,711	43,293	−13.1
Texas	139,046	159,487	171,449	171,665	172,085	168,897	161,580	159,234	−7.1
Utah	18,395	19,668	20,035	19,886	19,400	19,350	19,606	19,890	−0.7
Vermont	6,095	6,455	6,733	6,424	6,513	6,011	6,002	5,769	−14.3
Virginia	58,562	65,570	66,621	67,126	67,809	65,571	62,177	60,959	−8.5
Washington	50,425	50,990	50,402	50,046	⁴50,148	45,809	44,919	45,431	−9.9
West Virginia	26,139	24,631	23,369	23,580	23,589	23,561	22,613	22,262	−4.7
Wisconsin	66,753	70,979	69,332	67,743	67,357	64,321	62,189	58,851	−15.1
Wyoming	5,363	5,648	6,072	6,161	5,999	5,909	5,764	5,687	−6.3

NOTE: Data include graduates of regular day school programs, but exclude graduates of other programs and persons receiving high school equivalency certificates. They also exclude graduates of subcollegiate departments of institutions of higher education, Federal schools for Indians and on Federal installations, and residential schools for exceptional children. Some figures have been revised since originally published.

1 Revised from previously published data.

2 Preliminary data.

3 Beginning in 1983–84 graduates from adult programs are excluded.

4 Data estimated by the Center for Education Statistics.

Source: *Digest of Education Statistics, 1987*, table 71, p. 85.

High-School Dropouts among Persons 14–34 Years Old, by Age, Race/Ethnicity, and Sex: United States, October 1970, 1975, 1980, and 1985

Year, Race/Ethnicity, and Sex	Total, 14–34 Years	14–15 Years	16–17 Years	18–19 Years	20–21 Years	22–24 Years	25–29 Years	30–34 Years
October 1970								
All races								
Total	17.0	1.8	8.0	16.2	16.6	18.7	22.5	26.5
Male	16.2	1.7	7.1	16.0	16.1	17.9	21.4	26.2
Female	17.7	1.9	8.9	16.3	16.9	19.4	23.6	26.8
White								
Total	15.2	1.7	7.3	14.1	14.6	16.3	19.9	24.6
Male	14.4	1.7	6.3	13.3	14.1	15.3	19.0	24.2
Female	16.0	1.8	8.4	14.8	15.1	17.2	20.7	24.9
Black								
Total	30.0	2.4	12.8	31.2	29.6	37.8	44.4	43.5
Male	30.4	2.0	13.3	36.4	29.6	39.5	43.1	45.9
Female	29.5	2.8	12.4	26.6	29.6	36.4	45.6	41.5
October 1975								
All races								
Total	14.1	1.8	8.6	16.0	16.6	14.5	15.4	20.5
Male	13.2	1.6	7.6	15.5	16.4	14.0	14.4	18.9
Female	15.0	2.0	9.6	16.5	16.7	15.0	16.5	22.0
White								
Total	12.8	1.7	8.4	14.7	14.8	12.6	14.0	18.6
Male	12.1	1.4	7.3	13.7	14.5	12.6	13.2	17.4
Female	13.5	1.9	9.6	15.6	15.0	12.7	14.7	19.7
Black								
Total	23.4	2.6	10.2	25.4	28.7	27.8	27.9	36.8
Male	21.9	2.4	9.7	27.7	30.4	25.9	25.5	33.1
Female	24.7	2.8	10.7	23.4	27.3	29.2	29.9	39.6
Hispanic origin[1]								
Total	33.0	4.0	13.2	30.1	31.6	41.7	42.9	48.7
Male	29.9	1.9	11.1	26.3	30.2	40.0	40.6	45.0
Female	35.7	6.2	15.5	33.5	32.7	43.2	44.8	51.9

Year, Race/Ethnicity, and Sex	Total, 14–34 Years	14–15 Years	16–17 Years	18–19 Years	20–21 Years	22–24 Years	25–29 Years	30–34 Years
October 1980								
All races								
Total	13.0	1.7	8.8	15.7	15.9	15.2	13.9	14.6
Male	13.2	1.3	8.9	16.9	17.8	16.4	13.8	14.0
Female	12.8	2.2	8.8	14.7	14.3	14.0	14.0	15.2
White								
Total	12.1	1.7	9.2	14.9	14.5	13.9	12.7	13.4
Male	12.4	1.2	9.3	16.1	15.6	15.4	12.7	13.1
Female	11.8	2.1	9.2	13.8	13.4	12.6	12.7	13.6
Black								
Total	18.8	2.0	6.9	21.2	24.8	24.0	22.6	23.5
Male	19.0	1.5	7.2	22.7	31.3	24.9	22.1	21.9
Female	18.7	2.5	6.6	19.8	19.6	23.3	22.9	24.8
Hispanic origin[1]								
Total	35.2	5.7	16.5	39.0	41.6	40.6	40.9	45.4
Male	35.6	3.3	18.1	43.1	41.4	42.9	40.1	43.9
Female	34.9	7.9	15.0	34.6	41.9	38.6	41.7	47.0
October 1985								
All races								
Total	12.0	1.8	7.0	14.3	13.9	14.1	14.1	12.7
Male	12.3	1.6	6.7	16.3	14.9	14.9	14.2	12.5
Female	11.7	2.0	7.2	12.3	12.9	13.3	13.9	12.9
White								
Total	11.5	1.8	7.1	13.8	13.4	13.3	13.6	11.6
Male	11.8	1.6	6.7	16.3	14.2	14.2	14.0	11.5
Female	11.1	2.0	7.6	11.3	12.7	12.5	13.3	11.7
Black								
Total	15.5	2.1	6.5	17.3	17.7	17.8	17.5	20.5
Male	15.6	1.8	7.6	17.7	20.5	18.4	17.0	20.7
Female	15.4	2.4	5.4	16.9	15.3	17.4	18.0	20.4
Hispanic origin[1]								
Total	31.4	3.6	14.5	30.6	27.9	33.9	39.1	41.5
Male	32.1	3.2	10.1	42.2	33.5	33.9	37.6	41.1
Female	30.8	4.0	19.2	19.9	22.8	33.8	40.6	41.9

NOTE: Dropouts are persons who are not enrolled in school and who are not high school graduates. People who have received GED credentials are counted as graduates. Data are based upon sample surveys of the civilian noninstitutional population.

1 Persons of Hispanic origin are also included, as appropriate, in the white and black categories.

Source: *Digest of Education Statistics, 1987*, table 72, p. 86.

Year	Total Popu-lation	Age (Years)				
		Under 5	5–13	14–17	18–24	25–34
Estimates						
1950	152,271	16,410	22,424	8,444	16,075	24,036
1955	165,931	18,566	27,925	9,248	14,968	24,283
1960	180,671	20,341	32,965	11,219	16,128	22,919
1965	194,303	19,824	35,754	14,153	20,293	22,465
1970	205,052	17,166	36,672	15,924	24,712	25,323
1975	215,973	16,121	33,919	17,128	28,005	31,471
1980	227,704	16,457	31,080	16,139	30,347	37,593
1982	232,057	17,372	30,431	14,963	30,367	39,481
Projections						
Lowest series						
1985	237,605	18,046	29,581	14,691	28,628	41,662
1990	245,753	17,515	31,638	12,848	25,547	43,147
1995	251,876	16,193	32,193	13,932	23,347	39,887
2000	256,098	14,942	30,364	14,587	24,157	35,596
2010	261,482	14,298	26,525	12,814	24,605	35,511
2030	257,443	12,136	23,686	11,369	20,454	30,434
2050	232,222	10,553	20,437	9,573	17,391	27,337
2080	191,118	8,479	16,360	7,725	14,107	21,919
Middle series						
1985	238,631	18,453	29,654	14,731	28,739	41,788
1990	249,657	19,198	32,189	12,950	25,794	43,529
1995	259,559	18,615	34,436	14,082	23,702	40,520
2000	267,955	17,626	34,382	15,381	24,601	36,415
2010	283,238	17,974	31,888	14,983	27,655	36,978
2030	304,807	17,695	33,018	15,153	26,226	37,158
2050	309,488	17,665	32,583	14,600	25,682	38,383
2080	310,762	17,202	31,650	14,316	25,296	37,237

		Age (Years)		
35–44	45–64	65 and Over	85 and Over	100 and Over
21,637	30,849	12,397	590	(NA)
22,912	33,507	14,527	776	(NA)
24,221	36,203	16,675	940	(NA)
24,447	38,916	18,451	1,082	(NA)
23,150	41,999	20,107	1,430	(NA)
22,831	43,801	22,696	1,821	(NA)
25,881	44,493	25,714	2,271	25
28,144	44,574	26,824	2,445	32
31,913	44,555	28,528	2,673	36
37,570	46,136	31,353	3,202	50
41,500	51,699	33,127	3,811	66
42,972	59,859	33,621	4,444	84
35,554	75,626	36,547	5,486	140
34,679	66,600	58,085	6,490	233
29,537	61,057	56,336	11,088	408
23,863	49,630	49,035	10,085	551
32,004	44,652	28,608	2,696	37
37,847	46,453	31,697	3,313	54
41,997	52,320	33,887	4,073	77
43,743	60,886	34,921	4,926	108
36,772	77,794	39,196	6,551	221
40,168	70,810	64,580	8,611	492
38,844	74,319	67,412	16,034	1,029
38,222	73,748	73,090	18,227	1,870

(Continued)

Appendix Table A-30, Continued

Year	Total Popu- lation	Age (Years)				
		Under 5	5–13	14–17	18–24	25–34
Highest series						
1985	239,959	18,888	29,801	14,796	28,881	42,092
1990	254,122	20,615	32,935	13,120	26,137	44,329
1995	268,151	20,815	36,626	14,364	24,233	41,672
2000	281,542	20,530	38,128	16,306	25,326	37,850
2010	310,006	22,910	38,407	17,201	30,624	39,318
2030	369,775	26,562	46,999	20,567	34,190	45,739
2050	427,900	30,940	54,242	23,158	39,085	55,136
2080	531,178	37,439	65,466	28,236	47,911	66,393

Population in thousands. As of July 1. Includes Armed Forces overseas.

NA = Not available

Source: *Current Population Reports,* P-25, No. 952, table E, p. 7.

Age (Years)				
35–44	45–64	65 and Over	85 and Over	100 and Over
32,104	44,748	28,650	2,697	37
38,229	46,767	31,989	3,379	57
42,870	52,953	34,618	4,289	88
45,128	62,025	36,246	5,387	136
38,801	80,680	42,067	7,755	340
46,278	76,854	72,587	11,417	1,016
52,196	90,399	82,744	23,415	2,485
63,744	112,094	109,896	32,456	5,932

A-31 Projections of the Resident Population of Regions, Divisions, and States: 1980–2000

Region, Division, and State	Population			Percentage Change				Percentage Distribution		
	Census, April 1, 1980	Projections 1990	Projections 2000	Census[1] Change, 1970–80	April 1, 1970, to April 1, 1980[2]	Projections 1980–90	Projections 1990–2000	Census, April 1, 1980	Projections 1990	Projections 2000
United States	226,504,800	249,203,000	267,461,600	11.41	8.95	9.72	7.33	100.00	100.00	100.00
Region										
Northeast	49,136,700	48,423,300	46,400,600	0.16	−0.63	−1.66	−4.18	21.69	19.43	17.35
North Central	58,853,800	60,265,400	59,714,000	4.00	2.67	2.11	−0.91	25.98	24.18	22.33
South	75,349,200	87,594,200	98,827,800	19.96	15.42	15.92	12.82	33.27	35.15	36.95
West	43,165,200	52,920,200	62,519,200	23.90	20.46	22.20	18.14	19.06	21.24	23.38
Northeast										
New England	12,348,500	12,733,100	12,775,200	4.23	3.71	2.90	0.33	5.45	5.11	4.78
Middle Atlantic	36,788,200	35,690,200	33,625,400	−1.14	−2.01	−3.19	−5.79	16.24	14.32	12.57
North Central										
East North Central	41,669,700	42,371,800	41,646,600	3.49	2.20	1.39	−1.71	18.40	17.00	15.57
West North Central	17,184,100	17,893,600	18,067,300	5.25	3.82	2.85	0.97	75.9	7.18	6.76
South										
South Atlantic	36,943,100	43,144,400	48,974,800	20.42	15.88	16.51	13.51	16.31	17.31	18.31
East South Central	14,662,900	16,121,300	17,174,000	14.48	10.31	9.62	6.53	6.47	6.47	6.42
West South Central	23,743,100	28,328,500	32,679,100	22.86	18.06	18.90	15.36	10.48	11.37	12.22
West										
Mountain	11,368,300	15,404,100	20,139,900	37.13	32.93	34.96	30.74	5.02	6.18	7.53
Pacific	31,796,900	37,516,100	42,379,300	19.77	16.55	17.63	12.96	14.04	15.05	15.84
New England										
Maine	1,124,700	1,229,400	1,308,000	13.18	9.61	9.05	6.39	0.50	0.49	0.49
New Hampshire	920,600	1,138,800	1,363,500	24.80	22.94	23.37	19.74	0.41	0.46	0.51
Vermont	511,500	574,600	625,000	15.00	12.39	12.03	8.78	0.23	0.23	0.23
Massachusetts	5,737,000	5,703,900	5,490,400	0.84	0.74	−0.77	−3.74	2.53	2.29	2.05
Rhode Island	947,200	950,800	925,800	−0.27	−0.92	0.19	−2.62	0.42	0.38	0.35
Connecticut	3,107,600	3,135,600	3,062,400	2.49	2.71	0.70	−2.34	1.37	1.26	1.14
Middle Atlantic										
New York	17,557,300	16,456,700	14,990,200	−3.75	−4.93	−6.47	−8.91	7.75	6.60	5.60
New Jersey	7,364,200	7,513,100	7,427,600	2.69	2.47	1.81	−1.14	3.25	3.01	2.78
Pennsylvania	11,866,700	11,720,400	11,207,600	0.56	−0.18	−1.43	−4.37	5.24	4.70	4.19
East North Central										
Ohio	10,797,400	10,763,100	10,356,800	1.31	0.50	−0.60	−3.78	4.77	4.32	3.87
Indiana	5,490,200	5,679,300	5,679,200	5.67	4.47	3.13	−0.00	2.42	2.28	2.12
Illinois	11,418,500	11,502,500	11,187,500	2.77	0.42	0.45	−2.74	5.04	4.62	4.18
Michigan	9,258,300	9,394,300	9,207,600	4.24	2.69	1.16	−1.99	4.09	3.77	3.44
Wisconsin	4,705,300	5,032,700	5,215,500	6.51	7.31	6.66	3.63	2.08	2.02	1.95

West North Central

Minnesota	4,077,100	4,358,400	4,489,400	7.12	6.74	6.47	3.12	1.80	1.75	1.68
Iowa	2,913,400	2,983,300	2,972,100	3.12	2.36	2.13	-0.38	1.29	1.20	1.11
Missouri	4,917,400	5,076,800	5,080,000	5.13	2.67	2.99	0.06	2.17	2.04	1.90
North Dakota	652,700	678,400	682,000	5.65	3.93	3.60	0.53	0.29	0.27	0.25
South Dakota	690,200	698,500	687,600	3.59	0.25	0.90	-1.56	0.30	0.28	0.26
Nebraska	1,570,000	1,639,800	1,661,900	5.70	4.37	4.16	1.35	0.69	0.66	0.62
Kansas	2,363,200	2,463,400	2,494,400	5.07	3.86	3.96	1.26	1.04	0.99	0.93

South Atlantic

Delaware	595,200	629,800	638,200	8.60	5.87	5.51	1.34	0.26	0.25	0.24
Maryland	4,216,400	4,491,100	4,581,900	7.46	6.07	6.24	2.02	1.86	1.80	1.71
District of Columbia	637,700	501,500	376,500	-15.73	-19.93	-21.44	-24.94	0.28	0.20	0.14
Virginia	5,346,300	5,960,900	6,389,400	14.94	11.24	11.20	7.19	2.36	2.39	2.39
West Virginia	1,949,600	2,037,400	2,067,700	11.78	4.84	4.21	1.48	0.86	0.82	0.77
North Carolina	5,874,400	6,473,400	6,867,800	15.54	12.16	9.90	6.09	2.59	2.60	2.57
South Carolina	3,119,200	3,559,600	3,907,100	20.40	14.55	13.75	9.76	1.38	1.43	1.46
Georgia	5,464,300	6,174,600	6,708,200	19.10	13.06	12.64	8.64	2.41	2.48	2.51
Florida	9,740,000	13,316,000	17,438,000	43.42	37.43	36.55	30.76	4.30	5.34	6.52

East South Central

Kentucky	3,661,400	4,073,500	4,399,900	13.68	10.99	10.91	8.01	1.62	1.63	1.65
Tennessee	4,590,800	5,072,600	5,419,600	16.93	11.82	10.20	6.84	2.03	2.04	2.03
Alabama	3,890,100	4,213,800	4,415,300	12.94	8.77	8.01	4.78	1.72	1.69	1.65
Mississippi	2,520,600	2,761,400	2,939,200	13.70	9.04	9.18	6.44	1.11	1.11	1.10

West South Central

Arkansas	2,285,500	2,579,800	2,835,400	18.83	13.98	12.59	9.91	1.01	1.04	1.06
Louisiana	4,204,000	4,747,000	5,159,800	15.35	11.20	12.49	8.69	1.86	1.90	1.93
Oklahoma	3,025,300	3,503,400	3,944,500	18.20	14.77	15.48	12.59	1.34	1.41	1.47
Texas	14,228,400	17,498,200	20,739,400	27.05	21.72	22.54	18.52	6.28	7.02	7.75

Mountain

Montana	786,700	888,400	963,000	13.29	11.23	12.55	8.39	0.35	0.36	0.36
Idaho	943,900	1,213,800	1,512,200	32.39	26.63	28.02	24.59	0.42	0.49	0.57
Wyoming	470,800	701,300	1,002,200	41.63	40.19	48.26	42.90	0.21	0.28	0.37
Colorado	2,888,800	3,755,100	4,656,600	30.74	29.08	29.54	24.01	1.28	1.51	1.74
New Mexico	1,300,000	1,536,000	1,727,300	27.82	17.19	17.68	12.45	0.57	0.62	0.65
Arizona	2,717,900	3,993,700	5,582,500	53.08	46.63	46.46	39.78	1.20	1.60	2.09
Utah	1,461,000	2,040,300	2,777,400	37.93	38.46	38.73	36.13	0.65	0.82	1.04
Nevada	799,200	1,275,400	1,918,800	63.52	57.48	59.08	50.44	0.35	0.51	0.72

Pacific

Washington	4,130,200	5,011,800	5,832,500	21.00	19.12	20.98	16.37	1.82	2.01	2.18
Oregon	2,632,700	3,318,600	4,025,300	25.87	25.12	25.67	21.30	1.16	1.33	1.50
California	23,668,600	27,525,600	30,613,100	18.51	15.06	15.95	11.22	10.45	11.05	11.45
Alaska	400,500	522,100	630,700	32.35	23.10	29.66	20.80	0.18	0.21	0.24
Hawaii	965,000	1,138,100	1,277,700	25.34	18.53	17.49	12.27	0.43	0.46	0.48

Population rounded to hundreds. As of July 1, except as noted.

1 The census change represents the change from the April 1, 1970, census date to the April 1, 1980, census date.

2 The percent change April 1, 1970, to April 1, 1980, represents the change from estimates of the corrected population April 1, 1970, to the April 1, 1980, census date.

Source: *Current Population Reports*, P-25, No. 937.

A-32 Metropolitan and Nonmetropolitan Area Population—States: 1970–1985

Region, Division, and State	Metropolitan Area Population Total (1,000) 1970	1980	1985	Average Annual Percentage Change 1970–1980	1980–1985	Percentage of State 1970	1985	Nonmetropolitan Area Population Total (1,000) 1970	1980	1985	Average Annual Percentage Change 1970–1980	1980–1985	Percentage of State 1970	1985
United States	155,805	172,304	182,525	1.0	1.1	76.6	76.5	47,497	54,242	56,216	1.3	.7	23.4	23.5
Region														
Northeast	43,742	43,291	43,906	-.1	.3	89.2	88.1	5,318	5,844	5,953	.9	.4	10.8	11.9
Midwest	40,460	41,549	41,837	.3	.1	71.5	70.7	16,130	17,317	17,359	.7	—	28.5	29.3
South	42,282	51,489	56,813	2.0	1.9	67.3	69.4	20,531	23,883	25,045	1.5	.9	32.7	30.6
West	29,320	35,975	39,968	2.0	2.0	84.2	83.6	5,518	7,198	7,858	2.7	1.7	15.8	16.4
New England	9,822	10,020	10,230	.2	.4	82.9	80.8	2,026	2,329	2,431	1.4	.8	17.1	19.2
Maine	365	404	420	1.0	.7	36.8	36.1	628	720	744	1.4	.6	63.2	63.9
New Hampshire	404	511	560	2.3	1.8	54.8	56.2	333	410	438	2.1	1.3	45.2	43.8
Vermont	99	115	122	1.5	1.1	22.3	22.8	346	396	413	1.4	.8	77.7	77.2
Massachusetts	5,266	5,231	5,291	-.1	.2	92.6	90.9	423	506	531	1.8	.9	7.4	9.1
Rhode Island	868	878	896	.1	.4	91.4	92.5	82	69	72	-1.7	.9	8.6	7.5
Connecticut	2,819	2,879	2,940	.2	.4	93.0	92.6	213	228	233	.7	.4	7.0	7.4
Middle Atlantic	33,921	33,272	33,676	-.2	.2	91.2	90.5	3,293	3,515	3,522	.7	—	8.8	9.5
New York	16,647	15,869	16,091	-.5	.3	91.3	90.5	1,594	1,689	1,692	.6	—	8.7	9.5
New Jersey	7,171	7,365	7,562	.3	.5	100.0	100.0						—	
Pennsylvania	10,102	10,038	10,023	-.1	—	85.6	84.6	1,698	1,826	1,830	.7	—	14.4	15.4
East North Central	31,621	32,204	32,156	.2	—	78.5	77.2	8,642	9,479	9,486	.9	—	21.5	22.8
Ohio	8,565	8,521	8,467	-.1	-.1	80.4	78.8	2,092	2,277	2,278	.8	—	19.6	21.2
Indiana	3,551	3,719	3,737	.5	.1	68.4	68.0	1,644	1,771	1,762	.7	-.1	31.6	32.0
Illinois	9,125	9,339	9,488	.2	.3	82.1	82.3	1,986	2,088	2,047	.5	-.4	17.9	17.7
Michigan	7,361	7,481	7,291	.2	-.5	82.9	80.2	1,521	1,782	1,797	1.6	.2	17.1	19.8
Wisconsin	3,019	3,145	3,174	.4	.2	68.3	66.5	1,399	1,561	1,601	1.1	.5	31.7	33.5
West North Central	8,840	9,345	9,681	.6	.7	54.1	55.1	7,488	7,838	7,874	.5	.1	45.9	44.9
Minnesota	2,434	2,621	2,741	.7	.9	63.9	65.4	1,373	1,455	1,452	.6	—	36.1	34.6
Iowa	1,154	1,223	1,218	.6	-.1	40.8	42.3	1,671	1,691	1,665	.1	-.3	59.2	57.7
Missouri	3,170	3,226	3,301	.2	.4	67.8	65.6	1,508	1,690	1,728	1.1	.4	32.2	34.4
North Dakota	196	234	250	1.8	1.2	31.7	36.4	422	418	435	-.1	.8	68.3	63.6
South Dakota	155	180	198	1.5	1.8	23.2	27.9	512	511	510	—	—	76.8	72.1
Nebraska	650	708	747	.9	1.0	43.8	46.5	835	862	859	.3	-.1	56.2	53.5
Kansas	1,082	1,153	1,227	.6	1.2	48.1	50.1	1,167	1,211	1,224	.4	.2	51.9	49.9

South Atlantic	22,051	26,777	29,496	1.9	1.8	71.9	73.3	8,628	10,183	10,731	1.7	1.0	28.1	26.7
Delaware	386	398	413	.3	.7	70.4	66.3	162	196	209	1.9	1.2	29.6	33.7
Maryland	3,668	3,920	4,082	.7	.8	93.5	92.9	255	297	311	1.5	.9	6.5	7.1
District of Columbia	757	638	626	-1.7	-.4	100.0	100.0	—	—	—	—	—	—	—
Virginia	3,279	3,745	4,069	1.3	1.6	70.5	71.3	1,373	1,601	1,637	1.5	.4	29.5	28.7
West Virginia	683	718	710	.5	-.2	39.1	36.7	1,061	1,232	1,226	1.5	-.1	60.9	63.3
North Carolina	2,755	3,204	3,433	1.5	1.3	54.2	54.9	2,330	2,678	2,822	1.4	1.0	45.8	45.1
South Carolina	1,504	1,865	2,010	2.2	1.4	58.0	60.0	1,087	1,256	1,337	1.4	1.2	42.0	40.0
Georgia	2,807	3,403	3,816	1.9	2.2	61.2	63.9	1,781	2,060	2,160	1.5	.9	38.8	36.1
Florida	6,213	8,885	10,337	3.6	2.9	91.5	91.0	578	862	1,029	4.0	3.4	8.5	9.0
East South Central	6,913	7,903	8,195	1.3	.7	54.0	54.2	5,895	6,763	6,927	1.4	.5	46.0	45.8
Kentucky	1,550	1,677	1,694	.8	.2	48.1	45.5	1,671	1,984	2,032	1.7	.5	51.9	54.5
Tennessee	2,630	3,048	3,173	1.5	.8	67.0	66.6	1,296	1,543	1,589	1.7	.6	33.0	33.4
Alabama	2,169	2,462	2,558	1.3	.7	63.0	63.6	1,275	1,432	1,462	1.2	.4	37.0	36.4
Mississippi	564	716	769	2.4	1.4	25.5	29.4	1,653	1,804	1,844	.9	.4	74.5	70.6
West South Central	13,318	16,809	19,123	2.3	2.5	68.9	72.1	6,008	6,938	7,388	1.4	1.2	31.1	27.9
Arkansas	730	885	922	1.9	.8	38.0	39.1	1,193	1,401	1,436	1.6	.5	62.0	60.9
Louisiana	2,439	2,892	3,095	1.7	1.3	66.9	69.1	1,205	1,314	1,385	.9	1.0	33.1	30.9
Oklahoma	1,432	1,724	1,925	1.9	2.1	56.0	58.3	1,127	1,301	1,377	1.4	1.1	44.0	41.7
Texas	8,716	11,307	13,180	2.6	2.9	77.8	80.5	2,483	2,922	3,190	1.6	1.7	22.2	19.5
Mountain	5,155	7,263	8,316	3.4	2.6	62.2	65.0	3,135	4,110	4,473	2.7	1.6	37.8	35.0
Montana	169	189	201	1.1	1.2	24.4	24.3	525	598	625	1.3	.9	75.6	75.7
Idaho	112	173	192	4.3	1.9	15.7	19.1	601	771	813	2.5	1.0	84.3	80.9
Wyoming	108	141	146	2.7	.7	32.4	28.6	225	329	363	3.8	1.9	67.6	71.4
Colorado	1,772	2,326	2,623	2.7	2.3	80.2	81.2	438	563	608	2.5	1.4	19.8	18.8
New Mexico	456	609	686	2.9	2.3	44.8	47.3	562	694	765	2.1	1.8	55.2	52.7
Arizona	1,323	2,040	2,433	4.3	3.3	74.5	76.3	453	678	754	4.0	2.0	25.5	23.7
Utah	822	1,128	1,262	3.2	2.1	77.6	76.8	238	333	382	3.4	2.7	22.4	23.2
Nevada	394	657	774	5.1	3.1	80.7	82.7	94	144	162	4.2	2.3	19.3	17.3
Pacific	24,165	28,712	31,652	1.7	1.9	91.0	90.3	2,383	3,088	3,385	2.6	1.7	9.0	9.7
Washington	2,752	3,322	3,566	1.9	1.3	80.9	80.9	661	810	844	2.0	.8	19.4	19.1
Oregon	1,415	1,763	1,805	2.2	.4	67.7	67.2	676	870	883	2.5	.3	32.3	32.8
California	19,241	22,689	25,231	1.6	2.0	96.3	95.7	730	979	1,134	2.9	2.8	3.7	4.3
Alaska	126	174	236	3.2	5.8	41.8	45.3	176	227	285	2.6	4.3	58.2	54.7
Hawaii	631	763	815	1.9	1.3	81.9	77.3	139	202	239	3.7	3.2	18.1	22.7

1970 and 1980, as of April 1; 1985 as of July 1. Excludes Armed Forces abroad. Refers to 261 metropolitan statistical areas and 20 consolidated metropolitan statistical areas as defined by U.S. Office of Management and Budget, June 30, 1986)

— Represents or rounds to zero.

Source: *Statistical Abstract, 1987,* table 33, p. 27.

A-33 Projections of the Total Population by Age, Sex, Race, and Spanish Origin: 1990–2000

Age, Sex, Race, and Spanish Origin	Lowest Series			Middle Series			Highest Series		
	1990	1995	2000	1990	1995	2000	1990	1995	2000
Total population[1]	245,753	251,876	256,098	249,657	259,559	267,955	254,122	268,151	281,542
Under 5 years old	17,515	16,193	14,942	19,198	18,615	17,626	20,615	20,815	20,530
5–17 years old	44,486	46,125	44,951	45,139	48,518	49,763	46,055	50,990	54,434
18–24 years old	25,547	23,347	24,157	25,794	23,702	24,601	26,137	24,233	25,326
25–34 years old	43,147	39,887	35,596	43,529	40,520	36,415	44,329	41,672	37,850
35–44 years old	37,570	41,500	42,972	37,847	41,997	43,743	38,229	42,870	45,128
45–54 years old	25,226	31,044	36,533	25,402	31,397	37,119	25,578	31,763	37,813
55–64 years old	20,910	20,655	23,326	21,051	20,923	23,767	21,189	21,190	24,212
65 years old and over	31,353	33,127	33,621	31,697	33,887	34,921	31,989	34,618	36,246
16 years old and over	190,198	196,242	203,526	191,819	199,188	208,185	194,035	203,249	214,597
Male, total	119,620	122,608	124,671	121,518	126,368	130,491	123,698	130,577	137,163
Under 5 years old	8,964	8,288	7,647	9,827	9,529	9,022	10,550	10,653	10,508
5–17 years old	22,745	23,586	22,989	23,082	24,815	25,458	23,549	26,074	27,842
18–24 years old	13,016	11,904	12,314	13,127	12,072	12,530	13,283	12,325	12,881
25–34 years old	21,722	20,155	18,009	21,892	20,443	18,384	22,261	20,959	19,044
35–44 years old	18,598	20,649	21,508	18,732	20,879	21,866	18,927	21,322	22,537
45–54 years old	12,268	15,152	17,903	12,350	15,327	18,196	12,441	15,518	18,563
55–64 years old	9,804	9,733	11,046	9,871	9,865	11,272	9,936	10,000	11,511
65 years old and over	12,503	13,143	13,255	12,637	13,440	13,762	12,751	13,725	14,277
16 years old and over	91,205	94,152	97,779	91,929	95,480	99,906	92,964	97,378	102,913
Female, total	126,133	129,268	131,427	128,139	133,191	137,464	130,424	137,574	144,379
Under 5 years old	8,551	7,906	7,295	9,371	9,086	8,604	10,065	10,161	10,022
5–17 years old	21,741	22,539	21,962	22,056	23,703	24,305	22,506	24,915	26,592
18–24 years old	12,532	11,443	11,843	12,667	11,630	12,071	12,854	11,908	12,445
25–34 years old	21,426	19,731	17,586	21,637	20,077	18,031	22,068	20,713	18,806
35–44 years old	18,971	20,851	21,465	19,116	21,119	21,877	19,302	21,548	22,591
45–54 years old	12,958	15,891	18,630	13,051	16,071	18,923	13,137	16,245	19,251
55–64 years old	11,105	10,922	12,279	11,180	11,059	12,495	11,253	11,190	12,702
65 years old and over	18,850	19,984	20,366	19,061	20,447	21,158	19,238	20,893	21,969
16 years old and over	98,993	102,090	105,747	99,890	103,708	108,279	101,071	105,871	111,684

White, total	207,799	211,481	213,498	210,790	217,412	222,654	213,753	223,236	231,980
Under 5 years old	14,046	12,884	11,760	15,390	14,797	13,843	16,451	16,417	15,958
5–17 years old	36,028	37,062	35,876	36,523	38,941	39,667	37,149	40,716	43,061
18–24 years old	20,989	19,008	19,485	21,170	19,267	19,806	21,369	19,578	20,238
25–34 years old	36,027	32,867	29,009	36,289	33,312	29,590	36,768	33,998	30,442
35–44 years old	32,097	35,037	35,822	32,292	35,379	36,355	32,509	35,895	37,180
45–54 years old	21,868	26,822	31,239	21,994	27,077	31,662	22,090	27,286	32,071
55–64 years old	18,432	18,014	20,273	18,536	18,213	20,605	18,605	18,362	20,868
65 years old and over	28,313	29,787	30,032	28,596	30,424	31,126	28,810	30,984	32,162
16 years old and over	162,971	166,987	171,734	164,160	169,181	175,245	165,486	171,695	179,346
Male	101,518	103,352	104,369	102,979	106,266	108,879	104,460	109,175	113,536
Female	106,281	108,129	109,129	107,811	111,146	113,775	109,292	114,061	118,445
Black, total	30,836	32,506	33,957	31,412	33,651	35,753	31,974	34,780	37,602
Under 5 years old	2,948	2,771	2,620	3,215	3,165	3,079	3,440	3,525	3,570
5–17 years old	6,942	7,498	7,553	7,042	7,871	8,321	7,159	8,222	9,031
18–24 years old	3,766	3,495	3,715	3,798	3,542	3,773	3,849	3,620	3,865
25–34 years old	5,809	5,683	5,208	5,860	5,768	5,316	5,932	5,884	5,954
35–44 years old	4,254	5,096	5,701	4,295	5,169	5,811	4,339	5,261	5,479
45–54 years old	2,600	3,210	4,036	2,626	3,262	4,124	2,646	3,307	4,211
55–64 years old	1,978	2,035	2,292	1,998	2,073	2,355	2,013	2,103	2,407
65 years old and over	2,538	2,717	2,833	2,579	2,802	2,975	2,597	2,857	3,085
16 years old and over	21,922	23,230	24,996	22,138	23,618	25,613	22,372	24,055	26,317
Male	14,645	15,451	16,156	14,926	16,013	17,040	15,204	16,573	17,958
Female	16,191	17,055	17,802	16,485	17,638	18,714	16,769	18,207	19,644
Spanish origin, total[2]	19,148	21,149	23,065	19,887	22,550	25,223	22,053	26,475	31,208
Under 5 years old	2,047	2,039	2,033	2,282	2,412	2,496	2,690	3,129	3,510
5–17 years old	4,682	5,158	5,436	4,825	5,554	6,206	5,337	6,605	7,973
18–24 years old	2,289	2,376	2,602	2,386	2,511	2,766	2,811	3,069	3,499
25–34 years old	3,517	3,514	3,529	3,629	3,717	3,804	4,242	4,782	5,129
35–44 years old	2,721	3,309	3,602	2,788	3,430	3,803	2,900	3,771	4,590
45–54 years old	1,629	2,091	2,687	1,668	2,165	2,811	1,720	2,262	2,993
55–64 years old	1,160	1,297	1,547	1,183	1,341	1,619	1,209	1,394	1,709
65 years old and over	1,101	1,367	1,627	1,126	1,419	1,719	1,144	1,463	1,804
16 years old and over	13,070	15,663	16,434	13,453	15,322	17,419	14,763	17,597	20,807
Male	9,580	10,586	11,548	9,947	11,285	12,627	11,137	13,425	15,869
Female	9,568	10,562	11,516	9,940	11,265	12,596	10,916	13,050	15,339

In thousands. As of July 1. Includes Armed Forces overseas.

1 Includes other races not shown separately.

2 Persons of Spanish origin may be of any race.

Source: *Statistical Abstract, 1987*, table 16, p. 16.

A-34 Social and Economic Characteristics of the White, Black, and Spanish Origin Populations: 1985

Characteristic	Number (1,000)						Percentage Distribution					
				Spanish Origin[2]						Spanish Origin[2]		
	Total Population[1]	White	Black	Total[3]	Mexican	Puerto Rican	Total Population[1]	White	Black	Total[3]	Mexican	Puerto Rican
Total Persons	234,066	199,117	28,151	16,940	10,269	2,562	100.0	100.0	100.0	100.0	100.0	100.0
Under 5 years old	17,958	14,610	2,699	1,809	1,205	271	7.7	7.3	9.6	10.7	11.7	10.6
5–14 years old	33,792	27,417	5,218	3,355	2,249	516	14.4	13.8	18.5	19.8	21.9	20.1
15–44 years old	110,948	93,852	13,590	8,550	5,160	1,333	47.4	47.1	48.3	50.5	50.3	52.0
45–64 years old	44,549	39,033	4,406	2,407	1,227	372	19.0	19.6	15.7	14.2	12.0	14.6
65 years old and over	26,818	24,205	2,238	819	428	68	11.5	12.2	7.9	4.8	4.2	2.7
YEARS OF SCHOOL COMPLETED												
Persons 25 years old and over	143,524	124,905	14,820	8,455	4,755	1,241	100.0	100.0	100.0	100.0	100.0	100.0
Elementary: 0–8 years	19,893	16,224	3,113	3,192	2,062	417	13.9	13.0	21.0	37.7	43.4	33.7
High school: 1–3 years	17,553	14,365	2,851	1,210	700	248	12.2	11.5	19.2	14.3	14.7	20.0
4 years	54,866	48,728	5,027	2,402	1,243	347	38.2	39.0	33.9	28.4	26.1	28.0
College: 1–3 years	23,405	20,652	2,188	932	486	141	16.3	16.5	14.8	11.0	10.2	11.4
4 years or more	27,808	24,935	1,640	718	264	87	19.4	20.0	11.1	8.5	5.5	7.0
LABOR FORCE STATUS												
Civilians 16 years old and over	178,206	153,679	19,664	11,528	6,670	1,594	100.0	100.0	100.0	100.0	100.0	100.0
Civilian labor force	115,461	99,926	12,364	7,448	4,469	835	64.8	65.0	62.9	64.6	67.0	52.4
Employed	107,150	93,736	10,501	6,664	3,983	719	60.1	61.0	53.4	57.8	59.7	45.1
Unemployed	8,312	6,191	1,864	785	487	116	4.7	4.0	9.5	6.8	7.3	7.3
Unemployment rate[4]	7.2	6.2	15.1	10.5	10.9	13.9	(x)	(x)	(x)	(x)	(x)	(x)
Not in labor force	62,744	53,753	7,299	4,080	2,201	759	35.2	35.0	37.1	35.4	33.0	47.6

	Number						Percent					
FAMILY TYPE												
Total families	62,706	54,400	6,778	3,939	2,251	621	100.0	100.0	100.0	100.0	100.0	100.0
With own children[5]	31,112	26,232	3,890	2,602	1,543	447	49.6	48.2	57.4	66.1	68.5	72.1
Married couple	50,350	45,643	3,469	2,824	1,703	323	80.3	83.9	51.2	71.7	75.7	52.0
With own children[5]	24,210	21,565	1,822	1,892	1,207	218	38.6	39.6	26.9	48.0	53.6	35.1
Female householder, no spouse present	10,129	6,941	2,964	905	418	273	16.2	12.8	43.7	23.0	18.6	44.0
With own children[5]	6,006	3,922	1,942	642	302	213	9.6	7.2	28.7	16.3	13.4	34.3
Male householder, no spouse present	2,228	1,816	344	210	130	25	3.6	3.3	5.1	5.3	5.8	4.0
With own children[5]	896	744	126	68	34	16	1.4	1.4	1.9	1.7	1.5	2.6
FAMILY INCOME, 1984												
Total families	62,706	54,400	6,778	3,939	2,251	621	100.0	100.0	100.0	100.0	100.0	100.0
Less than $5,000	3,144	2,057	999	383	173	128	5.0	3.8	14.7	9.7	7.6	20.6
$5,000–$9,999	5,894	4,433	1,300	618	350	143	9.4	8.1	19.2	15.7	15.6	22.9
$10,000–$14,999	6,780	5,607	1,014	591	377	83	10.8	10.3	15.0	15.0	16.8	13.4
$15,000–$24,999	13,520	11,775	1,472	937	559	118	21.6	21.6	21.7	23.7	24.8	19.1
$25,000–$49,999	23,481	21,324	1,597	1,145	658	129	37.4	39.2	23.6	29.0	29.2	20.7
$50,000 or more	9,889	9,207	396	263	136	20	15.8	16.9	5.8	6.6	6.0	3.3
Median income	26,433	27,686	15,432	18,833	19,184	12,371	(x)	(x)	(x)	(x)	(x)	(x)
Persons below poverty level	33,700	22,955	9,490	4,806	2,904	1,106	14.4	11.5	33.8	28.4	28.3	43.2
HOUSING TENURE												
Total occupied units	86,789	75,328	9,480	4,883	(NA)	(NA)	100.0	100.0	100.0	100.0	(NA)	(NA)
Owner-occupied	55,845	50,661	4,185	2,007	(NA)	(NA)	64.3	67.3	44.1	41.1	(NA)	(NA)
Renter-occupied	30,943	24,667	5,295	2,876	(NA)	(NA)	35.7	32.7	55.9	58.9	(NA)	(NA)

As of March, except labor force status, annual average. Excludes members of Armed Forces except those living off post or with their families on post. Based on Current Population Survey.

1 Includes other races and persons not of Spanish origin, not shown separately.

2 Persons of Spanish origin may be of any race.

3 Includes other types of Spanish origin not shown separately.

4 Total unemployment as percent of civilian labor force.

5 Children under 18 years old.

NA = Not available.

X = Not applicable.

Source: *Statistical Abstract, 1987*, table 39, p. 35.

A-35 Population by Sex, Race, and Spanish Origin: 1980

Regions and Divisions States	Total	Sex		Race					Spanish Origin[2]
		Male	Female	White	Black	American Indian, Eskimo, and Aleut	Asian and Pacific Islander[1]	Other	
United States	226,504,825	110,032,295	116,472,530	188,340,790	26,488,218	1,418,195	3,500,636	6,756,986	14,605,883
Northeast	49,136,667	23,479,591	25,657,076	42,328,154	4,848,786	78,182	559,759	1,321,786	2,604,261
New England	12,348,493	5,923,926	6,424,567	11,585,633	474,549	21,597	81,005	185,709	299,145
Middle Atlantic	36,788,174	17,555,665	19,232,509	30,742,521	4,374,237	56,585	478,754	1,136,077	2,305,116
North Central	58,853,804	28,607,239	30,246,565	52,183,794	5,336,542	248,505	389,747	695,216	1,276,405
East North Central	41,669,738	20,235,410	21,434,328	36,138,962	4,547,998	105,881	302,748	574,149	1,067,794
West North Central	17,184,066	8,371,829	8,812,237	16,044,832	788,544	142,624	86,999	121,067	208,611
South	75,349,155	36,577,674	38,771,481	58,944,057	14,041,374	372,123	469,762	1,521,839	4,473,172
South Atlantic	36,943,139	17,870,778	19,072,361	28,647,762	7,647,743	118,656	260,638	268,340	1,193,823
East South Central	14,662,882	7,088,606	7,574,276	11,699,604	2,868,268	22,454	41,041	31,515	119,315
West South Central	23,743,134	11,618,290	12,124,844	18,596,691	3,525,363	231,013	168,083	1,221,984	3,160,034
West	43,165,199	21,367,791	21,797,408	34,884,785	2,261,516	719,385	2,081,368	3,218,145	6,252,045
Mountain	11,368,330	5,645,983	5,722,347	9,958,545	268,660	363,169	98,416	679,540	1,441,480
Pacific	31,796,869	15,721,808	16,075,061	24,926,240	1,992,856	356,216	1,982,952	2,538,605	4,810,565
New England									
Maine	1,124,660	546,235	578,425	1,109,850	3,128	4,087	2,947	4,648	5,005
New Hampshire	920,610	448,462	472,148	910,099	3,990	1,352	2,929	2,240	5,587
Vermont	511,456	249,080	262,376	506,736	1,135	984	1,355	1,246	3,304
Massachusetts	5,737,037	2,730,893	3,006,144	5,362,836	221,279	7,743	49,501	95,678	141,043
Rhode Island	947,154	451,251	495,903	896,692	27,584	2,898	5,303	14,677	19,707
Connecticut	3,107,576	1,498,005	1,609,571	2,799,420	217,433	4,533	18,970	67,220	124,499
Middle Atlantic									
New York	17,557,288	8,338,961	9,218,327	13,961,106	2,401,842	38,732	310,531	845,077	1,659,245
New Jersey	7,364,158	3,532,719	3,831,439	6,127,090	924,786	8,394	103,842	200,046	491,867
Pennsylvania	11,866,728	5,683,985	6,182,743	10,654,325	1,047,609	9,459	64,381	90,954	154,004
East North Central									
Ohio	10,797,419	5,217,027	5,580,392	9,597,266	1,076,734	12,240	47,813	63,366	119,880
Indiana	5,490,179	2,665,805	2,824,374	5,004,567	414,732	7,835	20,488	42,557	87,020
Illinois	11,418,461	5,533,525	5,884,936	9,225,575	1,675,229	16,271	159,551	341,835	635,525
Michigan	9,258,344	4,513,951	4,744,393	7,868,956	1,198,710	40,038	56,731	93,909	162,388
Wisconsin	4,705,335	2,305,102	2,400,233	4,442,598	182,593	29,497	18,165	32,482	62,981

West North Central								
Minnesota	4,077,148	1,998,406	2,078,742	53,342	35,026	26,533	25,299	32,124
Iowa	2,913,387	1,416,195	1,497,192	41,700	5,453	11,577	15,852	25,536
Missouri	4,917,444	2,365,827	2,551,617	514,274	12,319	23,108	21,476	51,667
North Dakota	652,695	328,409	324,286	2,568	20,157	1,979	2,455	3,903
South Dakota	690,178	340,370	349,808	2,144	45,101	1,728	2,250	4,028
Nebraska	1,570,006	765,902	804,104	48,389	9,197	6,996	14,855	28,020
Kansas	2,363,208	1,156,720	1,206,488	126,127	15,371	15,078	38,880	63,333
South Atlantic								
Delaware	595,225	286,998	308,227	95,971	1,330	4,132	5,249	9,671
Maryland	4,216,446	2,042,558	2,173,888	958,050	8,021	64,276	27,687	64,740
District of Columbia	637,651	295,039	342,612	448,229	1,031	6,635	9,960	17,652
Virginia	5,346,279	2,618,068	2,728,211	1,008,311	9,336	66,209	32,689	79,873
West Virginia	1,949,644	945,408	1,004,236	65,051	1,610	5,194	3,038	12,707
North Carolina	5,874,429	2,852,012	3,022,417	1,316,050	64,635	21,168	19,566	56,607
South Carolina	3,119,208	1,516,905	1,602,303	948,146	5,758	11,807	8,375	33,414
Georgia	5,464,265	2,641,030	2,823,235	1,465,457	7,619	24,461	18,721	61,261
Florida	9,739,992	4,672,760	5,067,232	1,342,478	19,316	56,756	143,055	857,898
East South Central								
Kentucky	3,661,433	1,789,330	1,872,103	259,490	3,610	9,971	8,714	27,403
Tennessee	4,590,750	2,216,395	2,374,355	725,949	5,103	13,963	10,657	34,081
Alabama	3,890,061	1,869,003	2,021,058	995,623	7,561	9,695	7,494	33,100
Mississippi	2,520,638	1,213,878	1,306,760	887,206	6,180	7,412	4,650	24,731
West South Central								
Arkansas	2,285,513	1,104,258	1,181,255	373,192	9,411	6,732	6,176	17,873
Louisiana	4,203,972	2,039,012	2,164,960	1,237,263	12,064	23,771	19,603	99,105
Oklahoma	3,025,266	1,476,719	1,548,547	204,658	169,464	17,274	36,087	57,413
Texas	14,228,383	6,998,301	7,230,082	1,710,250	40,074	120,306	1,160,090	2,985,643
Mountain								
Montana	786,690	392,625	394,065	1,786	37,270	2,503	4,983	9,974
Idaho	943,935	471,155	472,780	2,716	10,521	5,948	23,109	36,615
Wyoming	470,816	241,284	229,532	3,364	7,125	1,969	10,642	24,499
Colorado	2,888,834	1,433,737	1,455,097	101,702	18,059	29,897	168,561	339,300
New Mexico	1,299,968	640,643	659,325	24,042	104,777	6,816	187,868	476,089
Arizona	2,717,866	1,337,666	1,380,200	75,034	152,857	22,098	227,844	440,915
Utah	1,461,037	724,501	736,536	9,225	19,256	15,076	34,930	60,302
Nevada	799,184	404,372	394,812	50,791	13,304	14,109	21,603	53,786
Pacific								
Washington	4,130,163	2,051,369	2,078,794	105,544	60,771	102,503	84,049	119,986
Oregon	2,632,663	1,296,355	1,336,308	37,059	27,309	34,767	43,336	65,833
California	23,668,562	11,666,949	12,001,613	1,819,282	201,311	1,253,987	2,362,293	4,543,770
Alaska	400,481	212,321	188,160	13,619	64,047	8,035	6,325	9,497
Hawaii	965,000	494,814	470,186	17,352	2,778	583,660	42,602	71,479

1 Some Asian and Pacific Islander groups such as Cambodian, Laotian, and Thai are included in the "Other" category.

2 Persons of Spanish origin may be of any race.

Source: *1980 Census of Population,* PC 80–1.

Appendix   COMMUNITY COLLEGE FACT BOOK   **153**

A-36 Households—States: 1970–1985

Region, Division, and State	Number (1,000)			Average Annual Percentage Change	
	1970	1980	1985	1970–1980	1980–1985
United States	63,450	80,390	87,489	2.4	1.6
Region					
Northeast	15,482	17,471	18,410	1.2	1.0
North Central	17,537	20,859	21,647	1.7	.7
South	19,258	26,486	29,802	3.2	2.2
West	11,172	15,574	17,630	3.3	2.4
New England	3,645	4,362	4,665	1.8	1.3
Maine	303	395	428	2.7	1.5
New Hampshire	225	323	367	3.6	2.4
Vermont	132	178	195	3.0	1.7
Massachusetts	1,760	2,033	2,150	1.4	1.1
Rhode Island	292	339	360	1.5	1.2
Connecticut	933	1,094	1,165	1.6	1.2
Middle Atlantic	11,837	13,109	13,746	1.0	.9
New York	5,914	6,340	6,657	.7	.9
New Jersey	2,218	2,549	2,723	1.4	1.3
Pennsylvania	3,705	4,220	4,366	1.3	.6
East North Central	12,382	14,654	15,155	1.7	.6
Ohio	3,289	3,834	3,947	1.5	.6
Indiana	1,609	1,927	2,001	1.8	.7
Illinois	3,502	4,045	4,202	1.4	.7
Michigan	2,653	3,195	3,269	1.9	.4
Wisconsin	1,329	1,652	1,735	2.2	.9
West North Central	5,155	6,205	6,491	1.9	.9
Minnesota	1,154	1,445	1,533	2.3	1.1
Iowa	896	1,053	1,071	1.6	.3
Missouri	1,521	1,793	1,882	1.7	.9
North Dakota	182	228	242	2.3	1.2
South Dakota	201	243	253	1.9	.8
Nebraska	474	571	594	1.9	.7
Kansas	727	872	916	1.8	.9
South Atlantic	9,439	13,160	14,929	3.3	2.4
Delaware	165	207	227	2.3	1.8
Maryland	1,175	1,461	1,590	2.2	1.6
District of Columbia	263	253	254	-.4	.1
Virginia	1,391	1,863	2,063	2.9	1.9
West Virginia	547	686	707	2.3	.6
North Carolina	1,510	2,043	2,281	3.0	2.1
South Carolina	734	1,030	1,155	3.4	2.2
Georgia	1,369	1,872	2,140	3.1	2.5
Florida	2,285	3,744	4,512	4.9	3.6
East South Central	3,868	5,051	5,417	2.7	1.3
Kentucky	984	1,263	1,338	2.5	1.1
Tennessee	1,213	1,619	1,750	2.9	1.5
Alabama	1,034	1,342	1,438	2.6	1.3
Mississippi	637	827	891	2.6	1.4
West South Central	5,952	8,276	9,457	3.3	2.5
Arkansas	615	816	873	2.8	1.3
Louisiana	1,052	1,412	1,546	2.9	1.7
Oklahoma	851	1,119	1,237	2.7	1.9
Texas	3,434	4,929	5,801	3.6	3.1
Mountain	2,518	3,986	4,595	4.6	2.7
Montana	217	284	305	2.7	1.4
Idaho	219	324	349	3.9	1.4
Wyoming	105	166	180	4.6	1.6
Colorado	691	1,061	1,218	4.3	2.6
New Mexico	289	441	504	4.2	2.5
Arizona	539	957	1,158	5.7	3.6
Utah	298	449	506	4.1	2.3
Nevada	160	304	375	6.4	4.0
Pacific	8,654	11,587	13,035	2.9	2.2
Washington	1,106	1,541	1,677	3.3	1.6
Oregon	692	992	1,035	3.6	.8
California	6,574	8,630	9,820	2.7	2.5
Alaska	79	131	172	5.1	5.2
Hawaii	203	294	330	3.7	2.2

Source: *Statistical Abstract, 1987,* table 63, p. 46

	Number of Households and Families							
	Households[1] (in thousands)				**Familes[2] (in thousands)**			
		Average Population per Household					**Average Population per Family**	
Year	**Total**	**All Ages**	**Under 18 Years**	**18 Years and Over**	**Total**	**All Ages**	**Under 18 Years**	**18 Years and Over**
1940	34,949	3.67	1.14	2.53	32,166	3.76	1.24	2.52
1950	43,534	3.37	1.06	2.31	39,303	3.54	1.17	2.37
1955	47,874	3.33	1.14	2.19	41,951	3.59	1.30	2.29
1960	52,799	3.33	1.21	2.12	45,111	3.67	1.41	2.26
1965	57,436	3.29	1.21	2.09	47,956	3.70	1.44	2.26
1970	63,401	3.14	1.09	2.05	51,456	3.58	1.34	2.25
1973	68,251	3.01	1.00	2.02	54,373	3.48	1.25	2.23
1974	69,859	2.97	.96	2.00	55,053	3.44	1.21	2.23
1975	71,120	2.94	.93	2.01	55,712	3.42	1.18	2.23
1976	72,867	2.89	.89	2.00	56,245	3.39	1.15	2.23
1977	74,142	2.86	.87	1.99	56,710	3.37	1.13	2.24
1978	76,030	2.81	.83	1.98	57,215	3.33	1.10	2.23
1979	77,330	2.78	.81	1.97	57,804	3.31	1.08	2.23
1980	80,776	2.76	.79	1.97	59,550	3.29	1.05	2.23
1981	82,368	2.73	.76	1.96	60,309	3.27	1.03	2.23
1982	83,527	2.72	.75	1.97	61,019	3.25	1.01	2.24
1984	85,407	2.70	.73	1.98	61,997	3.24	.99	2.25
1985	86,789	2.69	.72	1.97	62,706	3.23	.98	2.24
				Series II Projections[3]				
1990 B	96,653	2.47	.67	1.80	68,619	3.01	.93	2.07
A	98,950	2.41	.65	1.76	68,816	2.97	.93	2.04
C	96,792	2.47	.67	1.80	67,325	3.04	.95	2.09
1995 B	103,856	2.39	.66	1.73	72,234	2.94	.94	2.00
A	107,528	2.31	.63	1.67	72,709	2.88	.93	1.95
C	104,194	2.38	.65	1.73	70,715	2.94	.96	2.01

Note: Figures shown are estimates and projections of civilian population of the United States plus members of the armed forces in the United States living off-post or with their families on-post. All other members of the armed forces are excluded. Alaska and Hawaii are included beginning in 1960. Data for 1940 and 1955 are estimates as of April 1. Data for other years prior to 1980 are estimates as of March 1. Data after 1980 are projections as of July 1.

1 A household consists of all the persons who occupy a housing unit.

2 A family consists of two or more persons related by blood, marriage, or adoption and residing together.

3 Three series of projections are shown for each year. Series B is based on 1964–1978 trends in marital status and householder proportions. Series A is based on series B and is calculated to provide an adequate upper range of variation. Series C is based on 1974–1978 trends for 1980 and on 1966–1980 trends for the other years.

Sources: ACE, *1986–87 Fact Book on Higher Education*, p. 10; *Current Population Reports*, no. 1, P-20, No. 411, tables 1 and 21, pp. 13, 14, and 21.

Money Income of Families—Percentage Distribution by Income Level in Constant (1935) Dollars, by Race and Spanish Origin of Householder: 1970–1985

Race and Spanish Origin of Householder and Year	Number of Families (1,000)	Percentage Distribution of Families, by Income Level			
		Under $5,000	$5,000–$9,999	$10,000–$14,999	$15,000–$19,999
All families					
1970	52,227	3.8	8.2	9.9	10.8
1975	56,245	3.3	8.9	10.4	11.1
1980	60,309	3.9	8.9	10.4	11.1
1981	61,019	4.3	9.1	11.3	11.0
1982	61,393	5.1	9.3	11.1	10.9
1983	62,015	5.2	9.2	10.8	11.0
1984	62,706	4.8	8.9	10.5	10.6
1985	63,558	4.8	8.5	10.2	10.5
White					
1970	46,535	3.2	7.1	9.2	10.5
1975	49,873	2.7	7.7	9.9	10.8
1980	52,710	3.0	7.6	9.9	11.0
1981	53,269	3.3	7.8	10.8	11.0
1982	53,407	3.9	7.9	10.5	11.0
1983	53,890	3.9	7.7	10.4	11.0
1984	54,400	3.7	7.7	9.9	10.5
1985	54,991	3.7	7.5	9.7	10.3
Black					
1970	4,928	9.9	17.4	16.2	14.0
1975	5,586	8.5	20.3	14.7	13.2
1980	6,317	11.4	19.3	15.3	12.2
1981	6,413	12.8	20.1	15.7	11.0
1982	6,530	14.4	19.9	15.7	10.6
1983	6,681	14.3	20.1	14.1	11.8
1984	6,778	14.3	18.8	14.8	12.3
1985	6,921	13.5	17.1	14.3	13.0
Spanish origin[1]					
1975	2,499	6.5	15.7	16.8	14.2
1980	3,235	7.1	15.6	15.7	14.1
1981	3,305	7.1	15.5	15.7	13.1
1982	3,369	8.2	18.1	15.2	13.3
1983	3,788	9.0	17.0	14.6	14.7
1984	3,939	9.6	15.3	14.3	12.0
1985	4,206	8.3	17.0	14.9	12.1

1 Persons of Spanish origin may be of any race.

Source: *Statistical Abstract, 1987*, table 731, p. 436.

Percentage Distribution of Families, by Income Level

$20,000–$24,999	$25,000–$34,999	$35,000–$49,999	$50,000 and Over	Median Income (Dollars)
12.2	22.9	19.3	13.0	27,336
11.2	21.1	20.0	13.9	27,421
10.6	20.5	19.5	15.1	27,446
11.1	19.6	18.9	14.6	26,481
11.4	19.5	17.9	14.8	26,116
10.7	19.2	18.3	15.6	26,642
10.4	18.7	19.0	17.0	27,376
10.3	18.6	18.8	18.3	27,735
12.2	23.7	20.2	13.9	28,358
11.3	21.7	21.0	14.9	28,518
10.7	21.2	20.5	16.1	28,596
11.2	20.2	19.9	15.8	27,816
11.6	20.1	18.8	16.1	27,420
11.0	19.9	19.3	16.8	27,898
10.6	19.4	20.0	18.3	28,674
10.4	19.2	19.7	19.6	29,152
11.6	15.8	10.7	4.5	17,395
11.7	15.5	11.2	4.9	17,547
10.2	14.9	11.3	5.5	16,546
10.2	14.8	10.4	4.8	15,691
10.2	14.8	10.3	4.2	15,155
9.6	14.3	10.2	5.7	15,722
9.1	13.3	10.9	6.4	15,982
9.0	14.3	11.8	7.0	16,786
12.1	18.9	10.8	4.9	19,090
11.4	16.8	12.7	6.4	19,212
12.9	16.2	12.9	6.7	19,399
12.0	15.3	11.7	6.1	18,085
11.6	15.2	11.5	6.5	18,280
11.7	16.9	12.8	7.6	19,505
11.3	16.0	12.5	8.1	19,027

Year	Total Non-institutional Population	Total Labor Force		Civilian Labor Force		Unemployed	
		Number	Percentage of Population	Total	Employed	Number	Percentage of Civil Labor Force
1950	106,645	63,858	59.9	62,208	58,920	3,288	5.3
1955	112,732	68,072	60.4	65,023	62,171	2,852	4.4
1960	119,759	72,142	60.2	69,628	65,778	3,852	5.5
1965	129,236	77,178	59.7	74,455	71,088	3,366	4.5
1966	131,180	78,893	60.1	75,770	72,895	2,875	3.8
1967	133,319	80,793	60.6	77,347	74,372	2,975	3.8
1968	135,562	82,272	60.7	78,737	75,920	2,817	3.6
1969	137,841	84,239	61.1	80,733	77,902	2,831	3.5
1970	140,182	85,903	61.3	82,715	78,627	4,088	4.9
1971	142,596	86,929	61.0	84,113	79,120	4,993	5.9
1972	145,775	88,991	61.0	86,542	81,702	4,840	5.6
1973	148,263	91,040	61.4	88,714	84,409	4,304	4.9
1974	150,827	93,240	61.8	91,011	85,936	5,076	5.6
1975	153,449	94,793	61.8	92,613	84,783	7,830	8.5
1976	156,048	96,917	62.1	94,773	87,485	7,288	7.7
1977	158,559	99,534	62.8	97,401	90,546	6,855	7.0
1978	161,058	102,537	63.7	100,420	94,373	6,047	6.0
1979	163,620	104,996	64.2	102,908	96,945	5,963	5.8
1980	166,246	106,821	64.3	104,719	97,270	7,448	7.1
1981	171,775	110,315	64.2	108,670	100,397	8,273	7.6
1982	173,939	111,872	64.3	110,204	99,526	10,678	9.7
1983	175,891	113,226	64.4	111,550	100,834	10,717	9.6
1984	178,080	115,241	64.7	113,544	105,005	8,539	7.5
1985	179,912	117,167	65.1	115,461	107,150	8,312	7.1
1986	182,293	119,540	65.6	117,834	109,597	8,237	6.9

All figures except percentages are in thousands.

Source: ACE, *1986–87 Fact Book on Higher Education,* p. 34; BLS, *Monthly Labor Review,* Vol. 110, no. 7, pp. 62–63.

Regions/States	1983	1985	Percentage Change 1983–1985	Regions/States	1983	1985	Percentage Change 1983–1985
New England	6,380	6,639	4.1	Indiana	2,584	2,735	5.8
Connecticut	1,608	1,711	6.4	Michigan	4,303	4,352	1.1
Maine	537	552	2.8	Ohio	5,110	5,130	0.4
Massachusetts	2,987	3,061	2.5	Wisconsin	2,435	2,374	−2.5
New Hampshire	503	537	6.8				
Rhode Island	477	500	4.8	**Plains**	8,567	8,862	3.4
Vermont	268	277	3.4	Iowa	1,422	1,416	−0.4
				Kansas	1,185	1,244	5.0
Mideast	20,062	20,559	2.5	Minnesota	2,174	2,234	2.8
Delaware	298	315	5.7	Missouri	2,350	2,472	5.2
District of Columbia	325	322	−0.9	Nebraska	788	813	3.2
Maryland	2,211	2,253	1.9	North Dakota	317	336	6.0
New Jersey	3,656	3,853	5.4	South Dakota	331	347	4.8
New York	8,062	8,308	3.1				
Pennsylvania	5,510	5,519	0.2	**Southwest**	10,806	11,749	8.7
				Arizona	1,026	1,477	44.0
Southeast	25,171	26,411	4.9	New Mexico	607	646	6.4
Alabama	1,761	1,803	2.4	Oklahoma	1,544	1,573	1.9
Arkansas	1,026	1,051	2.4	Texas	7,629	8,053	5.6
Florida	4,903	5,338	8.9				
Georgia	2,696	2,865	6.3	**Rockies**	3,470	3,558	2.5
Kentucky	1,702	1,695	−0.4	Colorado	1,667	1,720	3.2
Louisiana	1,910	1,987	4.0	Idaho	456	471	3.3
Mississippi	1,068	1,121	5.0	Montana	394	405	2.8
North Carolina	2,946	3,106	5.4	Utah	691	730	5.6
South Carolina	1,476	1,563	5.9	Wyoming	262	232	−11.5
Tennessee	2,189	2,245	2.6				
Virginia	2,722	2,872	5.5	**Far West**	16,922	17,612	4.1
West Virginia	772	765	−0.9	Alaska	229	253	10.5
				California	12,333	12,937	4.9
Great Lakes	20,025	20,264	1.2	Hawaii	473	481	1.7
Illinois	5,593	5,673	1.4	Nevada	487	509	4.5
				Oregon	1,337	1,327	−0.7
				Washington	2,063	2,105	2.0

Source: ACE, *1986–87 Fact Book on Higher Education*, pp. 32–33; *Statistical Abstract, 1987,* table 641, p. 377.

A-41 Employment by Broad Occupational Group and Selected Occupations: 1986 and Projected 2000 Low, Moderate, and High Alternatives (in Thousands)

Occupation	1986	Projected 2000 Alternatives			Change, 1986–2000 Moderate Alternative		
		Low	Moderate	High	Number Change	Percentage Change	Annual Rate of Change
Total employment	111,623	126,432	133,030	137,533	21,407	19.2	1.3
Executive, administrative, and managerial workers	10,583	12,900	13,616	14,105	3,033	28.7	1.8
Education administrators	288	316	325	336	37	12.9	0.9
Financial managers	638	747	792	824	154	24.1	1.6
General managers and top executives	2,383	2,820	2,965	3,052	582	24.4	1.6
Marketing, advertising, and public relations managers	323	402	427	444	105	32.5	2.0
Accountants and auditors	945	1,251	1,322	1,371	376	39.8	2.4
Personnel, training, and labor relations specialists	230	264	278	288	49	21.2	1.4
Professional workers	13,538	16,438	17,192	17,793	3,654	27.0	1.7
Electrical and electronics engineers	401	544	592	616	192	47.8	2.8
Computer systems analysts	331	544	582	607	251	75.6	4.1
Lawyers	527	676	718	748	191	36.3	2.2
Teachers, preschool	176	233	240	248	64	36.3	2.2
Teachers, kindergarten and elementary	1,527	1,778	1,826	1,883	299	19.6	1.3
Teachers, secondary school	1,128	1,246	1,280	1,320	152	13.4	0.9
College and university faculty	754	703	722	745	−32	−4.2	−0.3
Dentists	151	184	196	203	45	29.6	1.9
Physicians and surgeons	491	645	679	700	188	38.2	2.3
Registered nurses	1,406	1,951	2,018	2,077	612	43.6	2.6
Technicians and related support workers	3,726	4,884	5,151	5,325	1,424	38.2	2.3
Licensed practical nurses	631	835	869	891	238	37.7	2.3
Drafters	348	331	354	366	5	1.6	0.1
Computer programmers	479	758	813	850	335	69.9	3.9
Sales workers	12,606	15,522	16,334	16,760	3,728	29.6	1.9
Cashiers	2,165	2,616	2,740	2,798	575	26.5	1.7
Sales agents, real estate	313	422	451	468	138	43.9	2.6
Salespersons, retail	3,579	4,563	4,780	4,871	1,201	33.5	2.1

Occupation							
Administrative support workers, including clerical	19,851	21,028	22,109	22,885	2,258	11.4	0.8
Switchboard operators	279	313	330	343	51	18.3	1.2
Computer operators, except peripheral equipment operators	263	364	387	403	124	47.2	2.8
Bookkeeping, accounting, and auditing clerks	2,116	2,085	2,208	2,291	92	4.3	0.3
Payroll and timekeeping clerks	204	171	180	186	−25	−12.0	−0.9
General office clerks	2,361	2,688	2,824	2,916	462	19.6	1.3
Receptionists and information clerks	682	913	964	997	282	41.4	2.5
Secretaries	3,234	3,470	3,658	3,789	424	13.1	0.9
Typists and word processors	1,002	820	862	892	−140	−13.9	−1.1
Private household workers	981	883	955	970	−26	−2.6	−0.2
Service workers, except private household workers	16,555	21,051	21,962	22,562	5,407	32.7	2.0
Janitors and cleaners, including maids/housekeepers	2,676	3,144	3,280	3,380	604	22.6	1.5
Waiters and waitresses	1,702	2,360	2,454	2,503	752	44.2	2.6
Nursing aides, orderlies, and attendants	1,224	1,584	1,658	1,691	433	35.4	2.2
Hairdressers, hairstylists, and cosmetologists	562	627	662	683	99	17.7	1.2
Police patrol officers	349	400	409	422	61	17.4	1.2
Guards	794	1,104	1,177	1,241	383	48.3	2.9
Precision production, craft, and repair workers	13,923	14,722	15,590	16,225	1,666	12.0	0.8
Carpenters	1,010	1,134	1,192	1,252	182	18.1	1.2
Electricians	556	617	644	676	89	15.9	1.1
Painters and paperhangers, construction and maintenance	412	475	502	526	90	21.9	1.4
Plumbers, pipefitters, and steamfitters	402	452	471	493	69	17.2	1.1
Aircraft mechanics and engine specialists	107	122	129	130	22	20.1	1.3
Automotive mechanics	748	758	808	830	60	8.0	0.6
Machinists	378	345	373	385	−5	−1.5	−0.1
Operators, fabricators, and laborers	16,300	15,774	16,724	17,411	424	2.6	0.2
Sewing machine operators, garment	633	526	541	567	−92	−14.5	−1.1
Electrical and electronics assemblers	249	105	116	119	−134	−53.7	−5.3
Welders and cutters	287	284	307	320	19	6.7	0.5
Bus drivers	478	541	555	572	77	16.2	1.1
Truck drivers	2,463	2,821	2,968	3,050	505	20.5	1.3
Industrial truck and tractor operators	426	265	283	296	−143	−33.6	−2.9
Farming, forestry, and fishing workers	3,556	3,229	3,393	3,497	−163	−4.6	−0.3
Gardeners and groundskeepers, except farming	767	964	1,005	1,033	238	31.1	2.0
Farm workers	940	705	750	779	−190	−20.3	−1.6
Farm operators and managers	1,336	1,001	1,051	1,078	−285	−21.3	−1.7

Note: Data do not add to totals because of rounding.

Source: BLS, *Previews of the Economy of the Year 2000*, table 5.

Bibliography

American Association of Community and Junior Colleges, *Community, Junior, and Technical College Directory.* (Washington, D.C.: American Association of Community and Junior Colleges, 1976–1986.)

American Association of Community and Junior Colleges, "Fifty Years of Community, Technical, and Junior College Credit Enrollment," *Supplement to the AACJC Letter,* No. 234, March 24, 1987.

American Association of Community and Junior Colleges, *Supplement to the AACJC Letter,* No. 245, June 16, 1987.

American Association of Community and Junior Colleges, Tabulations, done in July 1987.

American Association of University Professors, "The Annual Report on the Economic Status of the Professor, 1986–87," *Academe,* March–April, 1987.

American Council on Education, *1986–87 Fact Book on Higher Education.* (New York: Macmillian, 1987.)

American Council on Education, Division of Policy Analysis and Research, Tabulations, done in April–July, 1987.

Astin, Alexander; Green, Kenneth; Korn, William; and Schalit, Marilynn, *The American Freshman: National Norms for Fall 1986.* (Los Angeles: Cooperative Institutional Research Program, 1986.)

Astin, Alexander; King, Margo; and Richardson, Gerald, *The American Freshman: National Norms for Fall 1976.* (Los Angeles: Cooperative Institutional Research Program, 1976.)

Bureau of Labor Statistics, *Geographic Profile of Employment and Unemployment, 1986.* (Washington, D.C.: U.S. Department of Labor, May 1987.)

Bureau of Labor Statistics, *Monthly Labor Review,* May and July 1987.

Bureau of Labor Statistics, *Previews of the Economy to the Year 2000.* (Washington, D.C.: U.S. Department of Labor, June 1987.)

Bureau of the Census, *Current Population Reports, Consumer Income Series P-60, No. 154, Money Income and Poverty Status of Families and Persons in the United States: 1985.* (Washington, D.C.: U.S. Department of Commerce, August 1986.)

Bureau of the Census, *Current Population Reports, Population Characteristics Series,* P-23, No. 150. (Washington, D.C.: U.S. Department of Commerce, 1987.)

Bureau of the Census, *Current Population Reports, Population Estimates and Projections, Series P-25 No. 1008, Estimates of the Population of the United States to June 1, 1987.* (Washington, D.C.: U.S. Department of Commerce, August 1987.)

Bureau of the Census, *Current Population Reports, Population Estimates and Projections, Series P-25, United States Population Estimates and Components of Change, 1970 to 1986.* (Washington, D.C.: U.S. Department of Commerce, various years.)

Bureau of the Census, *Current Population Reports, Series P-20, School Enrollment–Population Characteristics Social and Economic* (Washington, D.C.: U.S. Department of Commerce, various years.)

Bureau of the Census, *1980 Census of Population, Detailed Population Characteristics, United States Summary, Section A.* (Washington, D.C.: U.S. Department of Commerce, 1983.)

Bureau of the Census, *1980 Census of Population, Volume 1; Characteristics of the Population PC80–1.* (Washington, D.C.: U.S. Department of Commerce, 1981.)

Bureau of the Census, *Statistical Abstract of the United States: 1987,* 106th edition. (Washington, D.C.: U.S. Department of Commerce, 1985.)

Center for Education Statistics, "Associate Degrees and Other Awards Below the Baccalaureate, 1983 to 1985. (Unpublished Tabulations, May 1987.)

Center for Education Statistics, *The Condition of Education, 1985.* (Washington, D.C.: U.S. Department of Education, 1986.)

Center for Education Statistics, *Digest of Education Statistics, 1987.* (Washington, D.C.: U.S. Department of Education, May 1987.)

Center for Education Statistics, *Fall Enrollment in Higher Education.* (Washington, D.C.: U.S. Department of Education, 1976.)

Center for Education Statistics, *Higher Education General Information Surveys, Finance,* Fiscal Year Ending 1985. (Data tape, 1984–85.)

Center for Education Statistics, *High School and Beyond, Contractor's Report: Transition from High School to Postsecondary Education.* (Washington, D.C.: U.S. Department of Education, February, 1987.)

Center for Education Statistics, "High School and Beyond, Postsecondary Status and Persistence of the

High School Graduates of 1980." (Unpublished Tabulations, March 1985.)

Center for Education Statistics, "High School and Beyond: The Timing of Abnormal Progression among 1980 High School Seniors Entering Postsecondary in October 1980." (Unpublished Tabulations, July 1986.)

Center for Education Statistics, *High School and Beyond—Two Years After High School: A Capsule Description of 1980 Seniors.* (Washington, D.C.: U.S. Department of Education, 1984.)

Center for Education Statistics, *Projections of Education Statistics to 1992–93.* (Washington, D.C.: U.S. Department of Education, July, 1985.)

Center for Education Statistics, "Sample Survey of Estimates of Fall Enrollment." (Unpublished Tabulations, 1986.)

College and University Personnel Association, *1986–87 Administrative Compensation Survey.* (Washington, D.C.: College and University Personnel Association, 1987.)

College Board, *Summary Statistics, Annual Survey of Colleges,* 1986–87. (New York: College Entrance Examination Board, 1986.)

General Educational Development Testing Service, *The 1986 GED Statistical Report.* (Washington, D.C.: American Council on Education, 1987.)

National Assessment of Educational Progress, *The Reading Report Card.* (Washington, D.C.: U.S. Department of Education, 1987.)

Western Interstate Commission for Higher Education, *High School Graduates: Projections for the Fifty States, 1982–2000,* publication no. 2A129. (Boulder: Western Interstate Commission for Higher Education, 1984, and June 25, 1987, update.)

Index

The numbers in this index refer to the map/graph identification numbers appearing at the top of the pages, not to page numbers.